A Wild Woman in Borneo
Land of the Hornbills

By

Marcia Nightingale

Published by New Generation Publishing in 2019

First Edition

ISBN 978-1-78955-853-1

www.newgeneration-publishing.com

 New Generation Publishing

For my Dad
Geoff
&
Ting San

ACKNOWLEDGEMENTS

My main acknowledgement is to my Dad, Geoff, who has been my absolute champion, my inspiration and my driving force. You never gave up on me and drove me to write this book tirelessly for the last 12 years. Without your love and unending support this would never have come to fruition. I cannot express how much I love you and how much I valued your input and unerring belief in me. This book is for you Dad.

I would also like to thank Matang Wildlife Centre for the most amazing experience, which then put me on the path to volunteer at several other wildlife centres around the world, meeting some amazing, truly dedicated people out there, along with some wonderful fellow volunteers.

My friends Caroline and Heather for their input and advice during the final stages of writing, not to mention continued, and definitely valued, friendship.

Woburn Safari Park for allowing me time out from my job to go and live my dream for a while.

Sarawak Forestry for being at the forefront of forest management and conservation.

A final acknowledgement is in loving memory of Daniel Lloyd (also known as Taihg). A talented man sadly taken far too soon. Check him out on YouTube.

Some names in this book have been changed where I am not in contact with the people any more. Even though I have only used first names I felt this was the best approach but, of course, anyone who subsequently reads this book, recognises themselves and would like to be mentioned as themselves, then I am more than happy to edit the online edition, as well as any future hard copies.

Thank you all, you have enriched my life more than I can express and to say I have written a book as part of that process, certainly has a nice ring to it!

I must state that anything I have written is purely my own understanding and interpretation of my experiences at the time as a new and naive traveller. I had never worked abroad before and tried my best to fit in, understand and respect my surroundings but, inevitably, I may have got some things wrong. If I have I must apologise, as I would hate to cause any offence to anyone. My experience affected me deeply and still I think of my time there with fondness on a near daily basis. Part of my heart was definitely left behind in Borneo.

My intention in writing this book is, if I happen to make any profit from sales, I will be aiming to put those profits towards continual support of Matang in the hope it will continue to help local wildlife in need long into the future.

CONTENTS

"Travelling – it leaves you speechless, then turns you into a storyteller"

Ibn Battuta

CHAPTER ONE

"Life is short and the world is wide"
Simon Rowen

I was no different to many other animal keepers. You have your ideals and love animals. You want to give them the world, sometimes a world that they have never experienced, and are never likely to at the rate it is disappearing (in the name of progress, cheap products and short term mass profits).

The problem is that you can never achieve that world for them. I began my career in a Safari Park thinking this is a far better life for animals than a zoo where they are being stared at and laughed at, people banging on their windows demanding a personal show of some kind. As time passed I became increasingly frustrated though. At least in a zoo (a good zoo) they can now escape to hidden areas to find peace and have their own place, safe from humans. In a safari park people will risk anything for a photograph. Its not as if they are incredible photographers, as it is generally a quick snap on their phone. You would think a clue to visitors that these animals are to be respected would be the rangers who love and care for them, and who the animals know well, are patrolling in land rovers. We don't wander around amongst the lions, the tigers and the rhinos. Why then do you have to be constantly alert to people either getting out of their cars, just to get a little bit of a closer picture or, worse still, to have a picnic in the lion enclosure (this has happened)!! Other people are spotted holding their babies out of the windows for them to get a closer look. Theses babies are too young to know what they are looking at to be fair, and the animals....well, looks like a nice little tasty snack being waved in their faces. It wouldn't end well for anybody. The main human trait I would get most upset about, although you would have to admire the lengths some people would go to, is the insistence of feeding the animals with whatever they had to hand in their car. A car can hold so many items, not just the aforementioned picnic. I have seen primates being handed anything from soiled nappies and bottles of urine, to cigarettes and lighters, pens, drinks cans and chewing gum. As an animal keeper you would like to be able to utilise your time on patrol in a constructive way, watching and recording behaviours and hierarchies, learning about the species to further understand, respect and protect them. So much valuable data could be collected and researched in a safari type environment which could benefit both captive and wild animals. Just think how much easier it would be to rehabilitate and reintroduce rescued animals if we continued to learn from captive, free living individuals.

I have seen people actually turn up at the safari park and, just prior to approaching the entrance gates, absolutely covering their minibuses, people carriers and other large vehicles with smeared on food to attract the animals. Ladders have even appeared to ensure no part is left devoid of food. A single cheesy wotsit would be meticulously mounted on the top of the car aerial as a piece de resistance, like Master Thatchers fashioning a signature cockerel or suchlike as they finish a thatched roof. What people fail to grasp is that most of this food is actually harmful to the animals. We are left with very sick animals and sometimes having no idea what they have actually eaten in order to make them better. Another factor to consider is the high sugar content of many fruits and sweets is totally unnatural and can make animals hyper-active with "E" numbers. This then leads to fights and injuries, destruction of bonds within groups and general unrest. People cannot help but to interfere – they have to touch, feed, poke and generally make sure they are noticed by the animals they have come to see. What you are actually seeing then is very unnatural behaviours and learning nothing about these animals. The ideal visitor would feel privileged to catch a glimpse of a rare breed as it moved around its enclosure, taking time to just be, and watch these magnificent animals. Not making them ill, putting them at risk of injury and illness and teaching them to beg at the roadside. Very, very sad. Watching young macaques being born, raised by their parents, learning etiquette and survival techniques, and playing with other babies, developing characters, learning to walk and climb is one of the most awe inspiring things you can witness but to then see this diminish into them riding on cars, fighting over scraps and losing the shine in their eyes and the lustre of their coats is heart-wrenching.

The worst times for me were Bank Holidays when I would generally leave work each night with a blinding headache through stress and car exhaust fumes. The area I worked in was fenced all round so, although you were not particularly aware at the time, when you have cars crawling round 2 to 3 abreast in one big traffic jam you can only imagine the state of the air around the enclosure. Now, imagine you are a small monkey, sat by the roadside being coaxed by visitors, what height do you imagine them to be at? Exactly, car exhaust height!!

How I would long to be able to change these conditions for them. After all they had everything they needed for an ideal life - a perfect enclosure with grass, trees, log piles, ponds, enrichment treats, warm houses, balanced and plentiful diet, stable family and excellent health care. This all costs money and all these little guys have a job to do – to act as ambassadors for their individual species, educating people on how to help them survive in the wild (in-situ). You would hope animal lovers would be the only people attracted to these parks, where people come to gain an insight into these amazing animals. Sadly, this is not the case and the few who do spoil it for the majority, spoil it in a major way.

I loved these animals, they were part of my family. When they were hurting, I was hurting. I still think of them all daily. After a while I did become jaded, you feel you cannot make a difference, you are not getting the message across. I felt I needed to work in-situ and help rescue and rehabilitate primates, to get them back into the wild where they belong. So began the search for a volunteer placement, making sure it was a reputable Rescue Centre not something set up purely to make money from westerners by imprisoning animals unnecessarily (there are a fair few around!). During my search I found one that rang out to me. Their ethos matched mine. One main sentence just struck a chord with me, as if they were connecting with me personally, feeling my frustration with 'joe public'. It simply said:

"Before you touch an animal, think – is it for your benefit, or theirs"

That was it, that was exactly it. I had found my next step. The start of an incredible journey. The safari park I worked at were very supportive and offered me the chance of an unpaid sabbatical so I still had a job upon my return. Perfect. The trip was scheduled in the winter months, when the park was on restricted opening times, and I would also reap the benefit of escaping to a hot country.

A returning employee, Charlie, joined us at work on 27th September. He had been travelling and was looking to return to work again. It was perfect timing for both of us as he could fit back into my role (which had been his originally) and I was free to leave whilst the winter season was upon us. Many zoos and safari parks have a skeleton staffing level in winter months and increase with seasonal staff in the high season months. This day turned out to be a very special day, as a Totem object, to keep me safe during my trip magically came together too and was presented to me. I am very fond of first nations and indigenous beliefs and ways, so for a totem object to organically 'become', during that day of transition and handover, was perfect and felt so right for me. It just so happened I was given a small clump of Prezwalski horse hair, Charlie picked up some Colobus monkey tail hair and my line manager found a Chinese Water Deer tusk. All without any planning, purely coincidental at around the same time, on the same day. My partner cleaned them up, polished the tooth and combined the elements to make a pendant for me to wear around my neck. With all that love and energy it should be a very strong totem and my trip should run smoothly.

Thinking back now, what an amazing year I had had. At the beginning of the year, my sister had treated us both to a once in a lifetime trip to Swedish Lapland, to the original Ice Hotel at Jukkasjavi, where we saw the Arora Borealis. The temperature reached -35°C. Now, here I am at the end of the year, heading off to the rainforests of Borneo, where the likelihood of temperatures reaching +35°C are expected!!! Wow, talk about one extreme to the other.

So, volunteer forms filled in, information pack received and inwardly digested, flights booked, numerous jabs jabbed, passport and visa in place and phrase books handy I awaited the big day. Started Malaria tablets – although it turned out that my partner ended up having the weird dreams of huge plants, furry frogs and giant canaries and budgies! I was fine!

I was off to Borneo for 2½ months, volunteering with WOX (Way Out Experiences) at Matang Wildlife Centre, Sarawak, Borneo.

An important thread throughout my life has always been my love of music so, of course, I needed a soundtrack for my adventure. Again, Charlie came through with a recommendation from his recent travels. All backpackers were into Manu Chao at that time so that was a must. I also wanted some Yana Mangi songs (traditional Sami culture joik singing) from my time at the Ice Hotel, maybe thinking it would cool me down in times of intense humidity! I included other World Music and, most importantly ensured I had plenty of my old favourites and a compilation my niece Laura had put together, following our regular Monday meet-ups where we would both search and share new music treasures we discovered. A rare old mix but one which would prove to be very popular with fellow travellers along the way.

Another must do was to update the photos of my two nieces in my wallet – the current ones were of the girls in school uniforms and didn't represent the amazing young women they had grown to become at all! These were to be my 'daughters' during my travels into Asia. It was a recommendation when travelling in Asia during this time to not only hide the fact that I was gay but also to pretend to be married with children, especially at my age. This saved any hassle from some men and was the expected course of life, although I did still occasionally get a ribbing from men I came to know for not having sons, laughing and informing me that my husband "could not be very good to only give me daughters"! Whenever I travel I totally respect the cultures and laws of the country I am visiting, feeling thankful that I have the opportunity to visit in the first place.

MWC (Matang Wildlife Centre) is in the Sarawak state of Malaysian Borneo. Borneo itself is actually shared by 3 countries – Malaysia (Sarawak and Sabah), Indonesia (the Kalimantan province) and Brunei. Sarawak lies on the West Coast of Borneo, in the South China Sea.

My visit was in 2007 when Malaysia was celebrating 50 years of independence from British Colonial rule in 1957, celebrated on 31st August each year and known as Hari Merdeka (Independence Day)

"To my mind, the greatest reward and luxury of travel is to be able to experience everyday things as if for the first time, to be in a position in which almost nothing is so familiar it is taken for granted"

Bill Bryson

CHAPTER TWO

"The world is a book and those who do not travel read only a page"

Saint Augustine

It was 7am on the 9th of October 2007 and pouring with rain when Dad and Mum drove me to Heathrow – just right for rush hour too so I must make a note of that for future travel reference as it's very unfair on parents, especially when they are already nervous about you flying off into the unknown!

I was all set, my stomach wasn't churning like it was last night and my head no longer spinning or half as light as it was. Nerves had got the better of me and I had felt terrible, which worried me as I hadn't seen a hint of humidity or flown anywhere at that point!

Ginj, my partner, woke me at 4.45am with tea and toast and that was a great start to the day ahead. I had the numbers of 2 other volunteers travelling on my flight – Deb and Leanne which helped settle me too. WOX had organised this as an idea for volunteers to take up when travelling at the same time. I think its a great idea for any volunteer organisation to adopt as it gives you a good chance to get acquainted on the flight over, and stay on target with the complexities of travel, especially for people that have not done it before, and it creates an immediate bond ready to tackle the work ahead. Waving to Mum and Dad I entered the Departure area of Terminal 3. All went well and I met up with the others as planned.

Leanne worked in Marketing and was very efficient, with typed up labels and currency conversions and an air of confident Admin planning. She did however pack for every eventuality and had to pay £200 excess baggage! She had packed welly socks, trainer socks, walking socks - socks for every occasion.

Deb was more nervous and initially came across as a worrying hypochondriac, seeming to have pills for every eventuality. As I quickly discovered though she had a serious back injury and was actually really tough and determined, and some of the pills she had would be invaluable to us all. Much better prepared in that department than I was! She is an Archaeologist and used to doing really heavy manual work – loves to dig trenches apparently. Both proved to be really lovely, we all chatted quite easily and I felt close to them both very quickly during our experience. I would love to know what their first impression of me was, how I initially came across.

The flight to Kuala Lumpur (KL) was fine. I have always been a bad traveller (especially ferries and aeroplanes in turbulence) but I am very pleased to report that I didn't feel sick at all and the 11¾ hours went pretty quickly. Incidentally, Kuala Lumpur, the national capital of Malaysia, was founded in 1857 by Chinese tin prospectors and the name means "muddy confluence" apparently as it was built where the Klang and Gombak rivers meet.

The flight attendants were superb and kept feeding us meals and snacks, along with a constant stream of juice and water. I was hoping to see the famous Petronas Towers but sadly I missed them. These skyscrapers are constructed of steel and glass, with a skybridge between the two towers on the 41st floor. The Petronas Towers were once the tallest skyscrapers in the world, until they were taken over by Tapei 101 in 2004, and several others since then. Whether we were too high above the clouds, I was on the opposite side of the plane or that was the moment I lost my ring, I don't know. Because I did, unfortunately, lose a ring off my thumb, twizzling it around as I do. Of course, finding it would be pretty difficult as I was in the 'cattle class' section and with the plane coming in to land at the end of the flight, my ring could have rolled anywhere as it slipped out of my fingers and became lost under the seats and hidden amongst all the feet, shoes, discarded rubbish, pillows, baggage and carrier bags of duty free. I did stay on board to search for it once everyone else had got off but sadly no joy, I couldn't find it. I was so late leaving the plane the other passengers (including my new companions) had gone on to catch the connecting flight to Kuching. I wandered around looking for them for a while – my mobile phone constantly sending me texts inviting me to take on a sister connection, over and over! That was not helping me contact the others. Eventually, after realising I had missed everyone else heading in my direction, I asked at an information point where I needed to go. That was when I learned I needed to transfer to another terminal via a connecting train. I had a slight panic but it was absolutely excellent. Sort of between a tube train and a train carriage (very smart) and under two hoods inside the terminal. I just kept thinking of the famous bank advert "for the journey" with the cute little peanut headed people with long turned up noses in it and the accompanying operatic, beautifully ethereal tune, Eliza's Aria composed by Elena Kats-Chernin for the ballet Wild Swans playing in my head.

The journey to Domestic Flights terminal was a short one and I once more met up with the girls for our next flight. The second flight also passed by quickly. I think what helped was the personal TV stations had a language learning mode. I love to study so eagerly immersed myself into learning some Malaysian conversational words to set me off nicely. More food was handed out, although I don't really recommend Anchovy Curry for breakfast – not only because its a very odd breakfast option but it was an extremely hot curry too!

My first sighting of Borneo showed it to be flat, which was surprising. Shanties and oil palm plantations everywhere, and miles and miles of piles of logs.

Walking outside the airport was like walking into an oven but we had a driver waiting for us, again arranged by WOX, all ready to whisk us off to the hostel they had booked us into in the heart of Kuching.

Borneo residential areas are very similar to Bali – some REALLY basic housing and some really nice ones. The haves and the have nots very apparent in the styles of the buildings. Sarawak is a very rich state, the richest I believe, so the economy is booming, housing developments shooting up everywhere. After just 20 minutes or so drive, we arrived in the heart of Malaysian Borneo's capital city, Kuching, and our home from home, Singgahsana Lodge, No.1 Temple Street, situated perfectly for tourists, being very near to the waterfront area and major shopping plazas. Kuching is known as the city of cats, with many sculptures of cats around the city. This is because the Malay word *kucing* means cat. However, two other theories of how it got its name could be from the Chinese word *kochin,* meaning harbour or from the *mata kucing* tree as it is found all along the riverbank and bears a fruit known as the cat's eye fruit. Some of the architecture here is amazing and some of the buildings were funky multi-coloured art-nouveau styles – the multi-storey car park behind the hostel being one of them, with bright blue and green panelling and outline details of red, yellow and orange. Each floor had a different coloured balustrade. It all looked like a very elaborate birthday cake. The hostel itself, totally dwarfed by the multi-storey car park behind, was muted in comparison with only shades of orange brightening the exterior walls. Incidentally, this has now been adorned by the most amazing mural entitled "Wild About Kuching" and painted by local artist Leonard Siaw. It includes a picture of an orang-utan baby along with many other examples of local flora and fauna. It is 80ft wide and 3 storeys high. Well worth looking up on his social media pages.

As is customary, and good etiquette, all shoes must be left at the door in Singgahsana. Little wooden shoe boxes were lined up around the walls and any overspill left around this landing area. You then step **up** into the main reception area of the 'house'. Traditionally, Bornean houses were built on stilts, away from the dust and grime and you would climb up into the raised living area. People would sit on bamboo mats on the floor to eat and would sleep on bedding mats on the floor too. If you traipsed around your eating and sleeping area with dirty shoes, that could have all sorts on them, it would be very unpleasant to live in. Other reasons for removing shoes before entering the living space could be 'to leave the outside world behind', a way of switching off and relaxing as you come through the door. Also, it makes it a more peaceful space to wind down in, bare feet are much quieter than shoes and heels. Removing shoes is actually beneficial to your feet too. Reflexology points are stimulated when you walk barefoot - your feet can breathe, your toes can wiggle and no pressure from tight restrictive shoes. I am a big fan of this way of thinking, it has always seemed right to me, so I relaxed and felt at home immediately, which is the very ethos of this stunning hostel, owned by a lovely local couple, Donald and Marina Tan. An interview with them and wonderful images of their guesthouses can be seen on YouTube – search for "Borneo Inspired Guesthouse by Borneo Art Collective".

The Common Area was painted in warm oranges and yellows with potted plants, bamboo mats on a brown wooden floor and wooden bookcases full of books to borrow and board games to play. A small round coffee table surrounded by comfortable hammock style leather chairs lay in the centre of the room and to the right was a raised wooden platform with bamboo mats and cushions to relax on. In the far right corner was a small cafe area and a couple of computers with internet access, which could be booked by the half-hour. Traditional Sarawak crafts, antiques, paintings and photographs were found in all the rooms, lovingly collected by the owners on their travels throughout the years. Dormitories and private rooms were available starting at RM30 per night, which was about £4.50.

The 3 of us intrepid travelling companions shared a room containing two single beds and a bunk bed. The air conditioning worked fantastically and the ceilings were high, helping to take away some of the heat. The walls were orange and lime green, with fabric tapestries hanging on wooden poles. Western toilets and hot showers are provided, a luxury which we did not take for granted but did thoroughly take advantage of.

After freshening up we were eager to explore, so walked around Kuching, picking up local SIM cards to allow us to make cheap phone calls home. The shops sold wonderful wooden crafts and basketwork. However, pavements were a bit dodgy if you were elderly, disabled or if you had had a few drinks. Drainage gulleys about 4' deep ran along the side, mainly uncovered completely. Also, large pipework stuck out of the paths every so often, rather randomly. I later found this was common throughout places I travelled in Asia.

Returning to the hostel for a couple of hours' sleep we then planned to find a local place to eat. I did actually feel really rough and light-headed again, due probably to a mixture of heat, tiredness, anticipation and nerves. The short sleep helped and, once I forced myself up again, I was fine.

We found a nice vegetarian restaurant down a side street and we all ordered assorted dishes to combine and savour between us. I ordered a Mango Juice on the side but what actually arrived was a hot chocolate, which was a bit random, particularly in this heat! All very good though and around £4 for the lot.

Upon returning to Singgahsana we were rather embarrassed to discover we had missed an initial welcoming meal and meeting with Tim, the Project Manager. With the time differences, we had got confused as to what the **first night** actually referred to and hadn't been told upon arrival that it was arranged, or what time. All came good though when we met in the upstairs bar later and truly relaxed into our time there. It was indeed like one big family, a sanctuary where we would return on many occasions during our volunteer time. Most volunteers stay for 4 weeks but I had booked in for 9 weeks so would be fortunate enough to get more opportunities than most.

I loved the bar area instantly. It was up in the loft space of the hotel with bamboo matting on solid wooden floors. The ceiling was also covered in bamboo and had original Sarawak features such as leather and wicker pots hanging from the eaves. Solid wooden tables and benches gave plenty of seating of different styles, and little coloured mats everywhere. The roof had wooden shutters which opened from the bottom edge and were propped open with sticks, allowing fresh air in and giving stunning views out across Kuching's night sky. At one end, by the stairs, was a hammock and beyond that was a massive wooden bench, covered in a large bamboo mat, which had been built to slope back slightly. This big solid settee was positioned in front of one of these shutter windows giving you a personal cinematic screen of the skyline, facing the waterfront. There was a pool table in the main area I noted for future visits. Possibly my favourite features, although so hard to choose, were the written signs, hanging like bunting behind the bar which cited various inspirational and insightful quotes about travel, which you will see I have scattered liberally throughout this book, and the walls! Every wall of the bar was covered in scribblings from previous travellers. But it wasn't graffitti. These were personal thoughts visitors had wanted to share and immortalise. You could spend hours leisurely reading these thoughts, well only the ones written in English in my case anyway! What a lovely idea. Dates had been written underneath most of them so you could see the timeline of the atmosphere that had been created in this special little space above a hostel in Asia. I have never seen it since but think its a fantastic idea.

Richard, the brother of the owners, was on duty behind the bar and introduced himself. Such a friendly, warm and vibrant man, he made us feel REALLY welcome and instantly part of the family. Sadly, I heard Richard passed away in 2012. He introduced us to another group of English girls (who had done work with local tribes people). Tim and the other 3 volunteers joining us this time around Sandra, Jenny and Chris, plus Gill who is also doing a longer stint of 2 months like me, but who has done 1 month already. Finally, Aqil who is training to take over from Keith, the current volunteer co-ordinator and general manager of Matang, at the end of the year. A welcome couple of local beers and lots of chat, followed by a slot on the computer to send my first email home, before bed around 1.30am. No telling what I wrote mind you as, being late at night, the lighting in the communal area was dimmed and I hadn't got my reading glasses handy! Hopefully the message was understood and any blanks or nonsense I had typed could be filled in appropriately by the varying recipients back home.

Tim's conversation with me earlier was still buzzing in my head. He had asked if I would be interested in taking on the group of Pig-tailed macaques at Matang as a project, to enhance their enclosures and develop enrichment ideas. I couldn't believe it. My experience as a Primate Keeper had been noted and this, together with the fact that I was a more long-term volunteer, meant I had time to gain the trust of the animals and get to know their characters and their needs. I was being given the opportunity to really help make a difference. Tim trusted me and was allowing me the freedom to show what I can do. I was so excited and couldn't wait to reach Matang and get started. I may have slept a little but the time had come and I was ready.

"Two roads diverged in a wood and I – I took the one less travelled"

Robert Frost

CHAPTER THREE

"Half of the fun of travel is the aesthetic of lostness"
Ray Bradbury

B reakfast at Singgahsana Lodge the following morning was served in the bar area upstairs. It consisted of 2 slices of toast with jam, 1 banana, 1 glass of fruit juice and a cup of tea or coffee. A good start to any day. Tim picked us up around 9am and we drove the 35km to Matang Wildlife Centre, which is situated on the outskirts of Kubah National Park, right amongst the rainforest. The journey took around 40 minutes, and it was to be a journey we would come to know well during the next few weeks. The roads were excellent. Very wide and straight with drainage ditches either side to try to cope with the deluges of the rainy seasons. We passed a couple of large looking shopping plazas with decent sized Supermarkets, phone shops and open fronted cafes. The villages were well laid out, on a grid system it seemed, and schools looked modern and grand. Living in Milton Keynes I was well used to grid systems in roads. This was a main highway so traffic was constant with a high number of motorbikes and scooters. I noticed the riders all had their coats or suit jackets on backwards, flapping open at the back and later found out this was to prevent their clean shirts from getting dusty from the roads. Very clever. I imagine it would be virtually impossible to be able to do up your jacket at the back, it would end up being like a straight jacket!

After about 40 minutes of driving we took a left turn off the main highway and the large entrance gates to Matang (which translates as 'mature' I believe) appeared before us. Again, this was a wide, long, straight stretch of road, which had a very small shop set back a little way on the right hand side. This was noted for future reference as it was so handy and we were miles from the last shops we passed. I learned they stocked crates of beer and also soap which uses native ingredients and therefore supposed to keep mosquitos at bay. I foolishly never did buy some and try it, which may have been a wise move in retrospect as I had a particularly nasty experience with bites later on. The entrance to Matang looked very impressive and felt immediately welcoming. Driving through the gates a stream can be seen running under the road, which turned out to be much larger and deeper than I initially imagined. There was a car park and campsite area to the left but we turned right, to the staff quarters. This was a little micro village consisting of one short little road and 10 wooden chalets, 5 either side of the road, on stilts. This suited me perfectly as I have always longed to live in a log cabin in the woods with a verandah, near a waterfall or stream. I am in my own personal heaven. These houses do indeed each have a large seated verandah to relax in the evenings, either chatting with neighbours, reading a book, writing a diary or just enjoying the sounds and smells of the forest. There was a Papaya tree by the front steps of most of the houses. They were only small trees but I have never seen such massive Papaya (Pawpaw) in my life. It just shows how fruit is meant to look when grown in the right climate and natural conditions.

Inside each of the houses there is a large lounge, a kitchen/dining room, two good sized bedrooms, separate toilet, "shower" and sink areas. I put shower in quotation marks because we don't actually have a shower as such in our particular house – more a deep, tiled trough with a cold tap and a little bowl on the side. You wet yourself using the little bowl, tipping water over you either from the tap or from a larger container such as a bucket if you boiled up some warm water. Then rub your wet body all over with your soap before rinsing off with the bowl and water process again. This is an environmentally friendly version of a western shower, using even less water, which is a precious commodity that we tend to take for granted in Europe, but you learn to respect it hugely when travelling. This way of bathing is known as a 'Mandi' in Malaysia and Indonesia. Even now, when taking a shower at home in the UK, I respect and appreciate our fresh water supply and will take showers by wetting myself, turning off the water whilst washing, then turning on again to rinse. There is no reason to leave the water running while you are busy soaping. Its the same principal as leaving the tap running when brushing your teeth in my view.

A room, or in our case house, is known in Malay as a *bilik* and each bilik in the street has a name plate sporting the names of different native species of animal. Ours was called SLOW LORIS. I keep mentioning 'ours', I discovered I was sharing with just one other person, a long-term volunteer called Heather who has been here twice this year for prolonged periods (3 months so far this second time). We really hit it off well and I'm glad to be in just a 2 person Bilik as I am a little nervous until I get to know people. The other volunteers generally have 4 people in each. Once we had settled into our new homes Tim re-emerged and kindly gave us a complete tour of Matang Wildlife Centre (MWC) to introduce us to all the staff and animals and, although most enclosures are presently less than ideal, to give us an insight into the potential here and what the future could look like. The potential is in fact huge and the boardwalk path and steps winding around the rainforest animal trail, discovering the differing species in tucked away enclosures is idyllic, making me buzz with ideas all over again. However, at this present moment in time, as we wended our merry way around the boardwalk, we soon discovered that most of the enclosures were actually empty, devoid of any animals whatsoever. It transpired that some time ago one or more resident orangutans had managed to get loose and then go around freeing the other inhabitants! Matang had been built as a Centre Of Excellence for Wildlife care and you could clearly see this in the buildings and the design of the pathways meandering through the forest, enclosures tucked away amongst the foliage. However, it seems government cuts and reorganisations of the Forestry Commission had temporarily hampered the progress of this facility and it had quickly fallen into disrepair, with rusting locks and wire making breakouts for strong primate fingers relatively easy. WOX have now become involved and are here to work alongside MWC staff and the Forestry Commission to once again return Matang to its former glory and beyond, to work as a rescue and rehabilitation centre as well as being an educational facility for local and overseas visitors.

The animals resident here were still substantial however and included Orangutans, Gibbons, Macaques, Samba Deer, Sun Bears, Porcupines, Binturong, Civet, Buffy Fish Owl, Brahminy Kite, Lesser Adjutant Stork, Soft Backed Turtle, Leopard Cat, Salt and Fresh Water Crocodiles, a Cockatoo named Thea and several chickens (although these were a little more temporary residents, being a food source for the crocodiles etc)! The Lesser Adjutant stork was a very strange creature, its head would tilt right back, like a PEZ head if you remember those little sweet dispensers, and it would then appear to laugh, quite manically! They are not the prettiest of birds as they appear to have the body of a stork and the head of a vulture but they are highly intelligent and classed as vulnerable in the wild. It actually reminded me of Mr Burns in the Simpsons cartoons on TV to give you some idea.

The trees and plants around the centre are very well signed with interesting information on what each can be used for, such as furniture, hats, clothing, medicinal purposes etc. One very spiky plant could be played like a musical instrument as the spikes were hard and so could be plucked in such a way that they resonated and sounded a little like the African Mbiras, or thumb pianos (wooden boards with metal tines on)

As we were walking around the Pig-tailed macaque enclosure area, Heather, my room mate, appeared with a little orange bundle of wild hair and big eyes. This was Ting San, a female orangutan of about 2½ years of age rescued from the pet trade. They were heading back to the centre for lunch after spending the morning at their training platforms in the forest. Heather informed us

Ting San was making great progress. That day, she had apparently picked and eaten 5 different fruits from the trees. Whether she knew instinctively they were edible, had tested them out in a small amount to learn about them, or had learned from what little time she'd had with her mother (time unknown) and picked up the information that way, we don't know. Excellent achievement and rehabilitation step though.

The Trail was heavy going, with never ending steep steps in places – my breathing was heavy, my legs burned – but I kept going and did it, along with the others. I was very pleased with that, considering I'm not adapted to the climate, haven't slept properly for 2 days and have never been built for steep inclines. I had actually quit smoking a year beforehand and with the money I saved, gradually built up a home gym of workout equipment bought second hand. I then set to and worked out regularly in my own little home-made gym to try to prepare myself for the trip prior to coming. It will be good to see how I improve by the time I leave here!

The Macaque cage is awful, constructed of rusting steel and totally barren. Being on a hill it has a steeply sloping concrete floor running from the top where Emily the Bornean Gibbon is, down through the macaque cage, to the bottom. The only way of cleaning this is by spraying a hose through the bars, directing the water jet to force rotting food, banana skins, papaya skins and faeces down the hill to the end of the two enclosures. Of course, much of the debris gets stuck between bars separating the enclosure sections where it turns to a foul smelling, rotting, mush. No wonder the mesh and structure rust so badly. We were told the macaques do keep breaking out, as new areas of the enclosure become compromised. This seems to happen around once a month, when the macaques then spend their time wandering around the centre, before eventually heading back, to be let in for dinner. I can't wait to get cracking and make this an enclosure they will be happy to call home. Emily, the Bornean Gibbon (also known as Mueller's Gibbon), who's enclosure joined on to the back of the macaques, came over to see who we were. What a lovely gibbon she was too. Gibbons are part of the ape family, along with chimpanzees, bonobos, gorillas and orangutans, but are known as lesser apes and are much smaller than the others. All gibbons pair bond and sing lovely duets together with the male and female parts of the song being distinct from one another. They have no tail and very long limbs, using their arms to travel through the treetops via brachiation. This means they travel underneath the branches of the trees, grasping the branch with their hands as you would if you were using monkey bars in a playground or such like. Hence the name 'monkey bars'.

"For a demonstration of sheer exuberance, few animals can compete with a gibbon. To watch one swing extravagantly and effortlessly through the canopy is to witness an animal totally at one with its environment, and seemingly revelling in the fact that it can do something other species cannot"
Nick Garbutt, Wild Borneo (New Holland, 2006)

Bornean gibbons such as Emily weigh around 5-6½kg with the body and head measuring around 45cm in length and they are brown to dark grey in colour. I instantly fell for Emily, she brought back memories of my Nan, whose name was Agnes Emily, both having fluffy hair and heart-melting eyes. I made a promise to Emily then and there that she would also get an enclosure makeover before I left.

Once our tour of the complex was complete, Tim took us all to lunch and to a local supermarket at Matang Jaya, about halfway between MWC and Kuching, where we were each given our first 'allowance', to spend as we wished. This project is a self-catering project so you are given a certain amount of spending money to choose your own meals. This is a great way to become more immersed in the community, learn new foods and budget wisely. When you have never travelled to Asia before, you imagine tiny little shops and houses in small villages so I was very surprised to find supermarkets that rivalled our own, packed with anything you could need. The array of fruit and vegetables was amazing, although I didn't recognise many of them so became rather baffled by the choices. I was also amazed to find vegetarian diets were catered for far better than at home, finding mock duck and other delights in the freezer section. I would not have thought this would appeal to the majority of people here, most Asian diets being rice and vegetables but there is, as everywhere it seems, a large community of ex-pats so maybe there is a demand from this sector of the population. Needless to say, my shopping was a little random at best and not very successful as regards proper ingredients to make main meals with! I will get the hang of it I'm sure.

Back at the Bilik, I met Heather properly. We re-arranged the kitchen to accommodate my less than impressive shopping and Heather made a superb meal for us both, which I tried to take note of for future cooking reference. We sat on the verandah, chatting away the evening and I discovered the Bilik, my bedroom specifically, had been decorated just prior to my arrival. Something Heather had not had the pleasure of experiencing herself, even though she had been such a long-term volunteer with many responsibilities. This made me a little uncomfortable as I then wondered if they expected more from me than I had experience for, I was an Animal Keeper by trade but I had not reached the higher grades by any means. Heather was fine though and we both found it amusing but I did then vow to give my absolute utmost in repayment for their kindness. As the evening wore on, we were joined by a number of Geckos scurrying up and down the walls, and a bat flew into the house and then back out a couple of times. The constant buzz of the forest and the odd call of a bird is pleasant and not as deafening as I'd imagined, although down by the stream the sounds are completely different – it's just like when a telex is being sent, with the constant chirping of the cicada beetles (I think)!

The first night at the Bilik I was buzzing like the beetles too, and couldn't sleep again. I had arrived at my final destination and was being properly introduced to the rainforest as a terrific storm, complete with lightning, put on an impressive show nearly all night. The rain was rather loud on the metal corrugated roof, rather like being in a caravan on holiday in the UK when it rains heavily, but amazing nonetheless. What a welcome. After being mocked at school by my form teacher for several years I was now on my way to becoming 'the wild woman of Borneo'. He would call me this name constantly as I had moved from Northamptonshire to Buckinghamshire and, even though this was only about 20 miles up the A5 he insisted on calling me a 'northerner' and ridiculed my accent. Maybe I need to thank him for calling me the wild woman of Borneo, maybe this destination would never have crossed my mind otherwise. Funny how your life becomes mapped out. Thanks Mr Bull!

"And if travel is like love, it is, in the end, mostly because it's a heightened state of awareness, in which we are mindful, receptive, undimmed by familiarity and ready to be transformed. That is why the best trips, like the best love affairs, never really end"

Pico Iyer

CHAPTER FOUR

"Stop worrying about the potholes in the road and celebrate the journey"

Fitzhugh Mullen

I needn't have worried about setting my alarm – I awoke early the next morning to the territorial whooping of Emily, the gibbon on the hill, aimed at Theresa the other gibbon near the quarantine/office area. Also, hornbills (that had been released by Orangutans accidentally) were calling, to add to the morning chorus.

Our first day at work involved painting some black and white barrier fencing, as well as green metal sheeting panels for enclosures. Whilst painting we were given the task of coming up with ideas for a painting theme to decorate the new Sun Bear enclosure. We decided a mural of trees, blue sky, clouds and sunshine would be a suitable backdrop to try to make the enclosure feel even larger than it was for the bears. It was a very productive day and we all felt satisfied with our achievements and plans. Returning home in the evening I was then treated to a gorgeous chicken curry served with highland wild rice, cooked by Heather – absolutely beautiful. The rice was purple in colour and, like risotto, quite stodgy but I did enjoy it. Finishing off the meal was half a red dragon fruit each. I had never had it before and absolutely loved it. I believe it is from the cactus family and the skin itself does resemble the scales of a dragon. The colour of the fruit inside was a deep beetroot with tiny black seeds. I have since seen others in the UK (at an extortionate price) but these are the variety that are white inside, and just do not have the flavour. The red Dragon fruits are soft, with a mild scented type flavour and extremely refreshing. I would have many of these during my time here as a refreshing lunch or dessert treat (and sadly have never been able to have them since).

That evening we went over to Deb and Leanne's to finish off the day, chatting on their verandah. It seems they have already taken in some cats that have been hanging around the street, and bought cat food for them! All of us have obviously become a part of this place and feel totally at home instantly. Returning to 'Slow Loris' and ready for bed, Heather and I discovered we had an ant infestation around the kitchen sink. They are black and tiny, like thunderflies, but boy do they pack a punch! These ants can REALLY sting, even in water. Sleep would have to wait, we couldn't leave these little blighters to wander and spread anywhere else. We set about washing down and bleaching all the work surfaces, sides and floors to get rid of them. A couple of hours later, when we were sure they had been completely removed, we breathed a shared sigh of relief and said our weary good-nights.

Over the weekend we could hear the sounds of gunshots in Kubah National Park, which was upsetting. This is supposed to be a protected area but we were told that people go hunting in there, drunk or otherwise, and shoot the wildlife anyway, either for food or just for sport. This is concerning considering the resident Orangutans at MWC are working towards being released in this area.

This was the fifth day of my journey and I had a day off so I shrugged off these thoughts and decided to grab my camera and become a tourist, walking around the trails amongst the rest of the visitors. It was pretty busy being a weekend anyway but it was also the end of Ramadan so even more people were out and about, enjoying local amenities.

I walked all around the trail the way that visitors do, which is the opposite direction to how we walked it yesterday, so I could see Matang as it is intended to be viewed and hopefully trigger some ideas to help improve it. I really enjoyed myself and sincerely hope it will be able to be reinstated to its former vision as an outstanding rescue and educational centre for local people and visitors alike. The end of the trek culminated back at the centre where I was invited to join a BBQ that was in full flow and had been put on for us volunteers by the local workers. They are Iban people, but were celebrating the end of Ramadan fasting anyway, by cooking up a storm. I was informed that any excuse for food over here is a good excuse apparently, and people do seem to eat regularly throughout the day. The workers had cooked in the wood shelter out the back and the food looked amazing, all set out on palm leaves. We had fish baked in leaves with all different spices, chicken baked in 2-3' hollow bamboo sections, blocked with leaves at each end, pork and vegetables in other bamboo 'broilers' and roast pork. We also had tapioca leaves wrapped up in leaves, (resembling a pineapple shape and size) which were delicious. The roast fish parcels, tapioca leaves and bamboo cooked pork and vegetables were lovely but the roast pork, possibly wild boar, was all fat, rind and very chewy. The chicken in bamboo was also a very scrawny chicken as it was just bone and skin chunks. All was accompanied by loads of boiled rice and to wash it all down we were given drinks of orange squash.

They all kept telling us to "don't be shy" (*Ala Maloo*) and a great atmosphere with men, women and children all making us extremely welcome and at ease, despite knowing no English. We scraped by with a little Malay. It felt so lovely to be accepted as part of the family and the Matang team so soon. We in the UK are so reserved and we could benefit so much in life by just opening up and trusting a bit more.

After the meal, as everyone went back to normal daily routine, I returned to my Bilik, only to be invited to join some of the girls for a swim in the stream. I couldn't possibly refuse and am so glad I didn't. Although it was quite busy down there, the atmosphere was easy, the water just deep enough to cover you and relax in and was as clear as crystal, with fish swimming amongst all the rocks. Apparently there are crocodiles in the stream, but none have been seen for years. So that's OK then!

After drying off and changing it was off again to the centre to look at what they had in the way of enrichment objects and ideas for the animals.

Any animal in a captive environment needs mental and physical stimulation providing for it. In the natural world they would be busy exploring, searching for food, finding mates, socialising with others, the same as we would do in our daily lives. However, in a captive situation they do not have this luxury unless we provide it for them. Imagine you spend all day in a small room with nothing to do – no TV, no books, no games, no phone, nothing. You have no way of getting out and the only time you can eat is when someone pokes some food, of their choosing, through the door for you a couple of times a day. I am sure you would be stir crazy within a couple of days and stress soon leads to ill health. In order to keep captive animals healthy we need to be able to stimulate their senses and their brains, try to replicate their daily time budgets such as how long do they spend foraging for food? Which muscles would they need to use to access the food? Is the food high up or low down? What percentage of meat, fruit or vegetables needs to be in their diet to maintain natural levels? How do they need to move around the enclosure and at what level? Do they need mates or are they better alone? So many more things to consider. But this is where 'enrichment' comes in. We need to enrich their lives with items that keep them busy and entertained whilst meeting natural instinctive behaviours and needs for each particular species. It is an engrossing and fascinating field of animal work to go into and can become all encompassing – your brain constantly thinking of new puzzle feeders or ways to hide food so they can forage, different 'toys' to manipulate or enclosure furniture to install to create a 3D world to be explored, keeping the body toned and healthy. It is important to note that where an animal is likely to be released back into the wild it is crucial not to use man-made items, only naturally foraged ones to ensure they will survive when released, recognising the items we have provided from their habitat and so they do not approach homes where man-made products can be found. The jungle is full of everything you need to come up with so many different ideas for enrichment. Items such as leaves, wood, vines and fibres, grasses, natural fruits, berries and vegetation, shells and husks.

There are 2 types of Enrichment – Behavioural (**how** they spend their time) and Environmental (**where** they spend their time) and both of these need to be catered for every day.

A complete programme of behavioural enrichment had been devised, excellently documented and set up by Laura, a previous longer term volunteer. However, no-one seems to have the time to do enrichment at the moment. Baby Ting San is a full-time undertaking for one person and there is so much painting still to do in order to make bigger, better and safer enclosures available for animals currently in very poor conditions. The humidity and wet in the rainforest areas must play a large part in the degrading of mesh etc also. It must rust a lot quicker here.

Volunteers also have the daily duties of cleaning out Ting San's bedroom whilst she is out in the forest, cleaning the quarantine cages of the 3 individual macaques who can be moved into small inner safety cages by the local keepers, giving us access to their areas, and the two Samba deer (Tim and Simon) who are safe to go in with. Keith suggested I take on the role of Enrichment Officer full time and teach other volunteers and keepers in turn. I gladly accepted the challenge although, as we can't enter most of the cages for safety reasons (both for us and the animals), we are very limited as to what we could do. The local keepers do go into enclosures that we cannot but trying to get across the need for taking the enrichment in with them when they clean them out, and what the intent of those items is, can be tricky to achieve. This was going to be some challenge to ensure the enrichment is enjoyable, long-lasting and beneficial to the animals.

My first volunteers to help me out were my two trusty travel buddies, Leanne and Deb and, although we only did some quick enrichment to start the ball rolling, they both absolutely loved it and became totally inspired. The Quarantine monkeys and bears sprang into life with objects we had conjured up, making it all very worthwhile and satisfying for them. Considering they have nothing to occupy them in their small, practically empty enclosures I must admit that any change to their day is hugely appreciated. They are not actually in quarantine but the only available place for them to live at the moment is in the quarantine block, which is why it is totally unsuitable. Quarantine areas by nature are built to be a temporary, stark, clinical area to assess incoming animals and treat their health issues.

The gibbons and forest cat were not as successful on the enrichment front, not being very enamoured with their offerings. I didn't really think they would be though, as all we had to use were scraps of dinner food from staff, which is not at all suitable but needed using, and better than nothing. At the end of the day I grabbed the Behavioural Enrichment folders and took them back home to study, inwardly digest and build upon.

Our little village population was thin on the ground this evening. It was the birthday of Simon, a long term volunteer in Borneo, and at Matang in particular, so Heather was away in Kuching for the night, helping him to celebrate. Tim (you can now see where the Samba Deer got their names!) had also taken Sandra, Chris and

Deb into Kuching to watch the England Rugby match. This didn't appeal to me so I stayed behind and attempted to cook myself a dinner. I failed miserably by totally overdoing my rice dinner in every way. I cooked up way too much rice and cooked it for way too long, resulting in a huge stodgy purple heap!! YUK! At least I can use the rice as part of an enrichment treat tomorrow. Maybe make it into garlic rice or coconut rice and stuff leaf parcels or something similar which can be thrown onto the top of the enclosures or attached to the sides with coconut husk string for the macaques to manipulate through the bars. Leanne and Jenny had also stayed behind so they both came over to chat for a while and we noticed we seemed to be getting more and more geckos, which helps to keep the insect population down enormously. I love the way they just stick to the walls, like cat burglars, freezing, caught in the act, and the little sounds they make too – 'Eh Oh', almost as if they are saying Ge-cko over and over. Very cute. Maybe that's where the Teletubbies got their greeting from!

As volunteers we are generally not expected to work the weekends, but this weekend is a busy one and we all wanted to chip in, especially as we have only just started our stint here. I worked the morning with Jenny, cleaning out Ting San's bedroom and chatting to Simon about enrichment. Apparently its his 49th birthday today but he only looks in his 30s. Bornean life obviously agrees with him. We get a couple of hours for lunch every day, so I had an hours sleep as I was so tired this morning. I haven't been tired at all as I am just so excited to be here, working in-situ on my first project, but the preparation, the journey and the heat finally seem to have caught up with me now. As a quick lunch I fried the other lump of my stodgy rice mountain from yesterday. It improved it a little bit, but not much! The remainder was made into rice parcels in leaves for the animals. The afternoon was spent at the Centre, watching the resident Orangutans and enriching the Sun Bears and various macaques. Sun Bears are the largest carnivore in Borneo, but they are the smallest of all the bear species, weighing around 65kg and standing around 5ft tall. They have an orange or white 'bib' on their front, said to resemble the rising Sun, hence the name Sun Bear, but this can sometimes only look like a V or a C shape. They are also known as honey bears as they eat honey, along with termites, lizards, birds, fruits, berries and rodents. They are generally nocturnal and make nests to sleep in during the day, similar to Orangutans, although not quite as accomplished! At Matang we have Bernie, Situ, Jo and Corinne, currently in quarantine 'cells' and waiting for us to finish their proper outdoor enclosure plus Gummy Bear and another 3 in an outside enclosure which is far more natural and not bad at all.

Before the day was finished, I felt brave and, despite the smell, I held my nose and tried a tiny bit of Durian fruit someone had brought in. Not impressed at all I must say! It's like creamy, garlicky, rotten onion with the texture of raw, chewy, chicken skin – Yuk! I couldn't get rid of the taste. Apparently, if you follow up the fruit with a drink of water from the durian shell it stops your breath stinking. I wasn't going to risk any more of its delights though. Everyone who lives here apparently sees it as a huge delicacy and go mad for it. You are generally not allowed to carry Durian in taxis though, or have it in your room in many hotels, because the smell is so putrid and lingers for so long. Not really selling it to you am I?!

Caroline was in today so we got a chance to meet her for the first time. Caroline and Keith have both been responsible for running Matang over the past 2 years, and both are from the UK. She seems a really nice, gentle person and again, I took to her straight away, feeling we would have some great conversations about animal welfare and education in the future.

It seems Mamu, a baby Orangutan (and daughter of Chiam), has learned how to squeeze out of her enclosure through the bars, being only a small Orangutan. We watched as she promptly made her way along the wall to visit Doris, another resident orang, in her adjoining outside enclosure. Doris carefully helped Mamu down from the wall and they had a wonderful afternoon playing. Apparently this is a new trick Mamu has discovered and only the second time she's done it. The first time she got through the bars, she just whimpered until, with a little guidance from her mum, she managed to climb back through. This hadn't put her off though it appears, and this time she decided to go for it. We were so privileged to see this interaction. Great enrichment for both Mamu and Doris. Enrichment time proper was then upon us once again for the rest of the centre so I helped give out banana leaves to macaques, bears, porcupine and gibbons with Simon, a bit of a quick enrichment but still something they could manipulate, eat or build nests with as they pleased. Banana leaves grow in abundance around the forest but none of the enclosures have the trees growing in them. This could be because either they were cleared to build the enclosures themselves, they have been destroyed by the residents in the enclosure or they would have been useful to climb and therefore escape from said enclosure!

Having returned to the centre we found ourselves once more being invited to another Ramadan meal – this time at our neighbour's house, next door to Heather and I. He is the Site Manager of MWC working for Sarawak Forestry Commission. I had smelled it all cooking when I had returned home lunchtime and I must say the aromas had been wonderful, drifting across to tease my nostrils as I looked at my usual uninspiring effort I had prepared for myself. To be invited to eat this amazing food was readily accepted I must say and it was absolutely sensational - far, far better than anything I've ever cooked, or ever hoped to!

When the time came we all made our way round to the house. "Selamat Hari Raya" and "Terima Kase" - lots more "Ala Maloo's" and we all tucked in. Some guests came in traditional tunic and long skirt sets – really pretty. James, Matangs' animal manager, Leah his wife and their 3 kids came too. The feast consisted of rice cooked in bamboo, plain flattened rice and biriani rice, beef randan curry and chicken curry. Also little cakes and sweets. One cake, like a malted slab and known as Stingray Heart, apparently takes 8 hours to cook. We were also offered these little red berries which were out of this world. They tasted like glace cherries and almond, sort of a bakewell tart tasting berry. I vowed I must find out what they were called and go get me some but sadly never did discover what they were. I noticed that wives will spend all day cooking but will not begin to eat until we have all had our fill. They would just slip back behind the brightly coloured curtains into the kitchen to continue preparing dish after dish. What a wonderful treat. We were so honoured to be invited and the evening just flew by in an explosion of colour, taste and smell sensations.

Returning to 'Slow Loris' it was time to have a Mandi before doing some washing and, later on, welcoming Heather home from her trip to Kuching, swapping our tales of the weekend as we sat on the verandah.

Morning duties the following day consisted of cleaning out Ting San's bedroom and painting yet more metal sheeting for the Orangutan nursery enclosure. Ice block enrichment was the order of the day, lovely treaty bits that are frozen in ice blocks to release the treats slowly, keeping the animals mentally and physically active, working for their food, and also cooling them down in the humid heat. Come the afternoon it was lashing it down with rain so Keith enlisted our help, working under the shelter of the workshop, to saw some wood with him. He is making press feeders for the primates, the same as you would find in zoos in the UK. These are like flower presses, consisting of a wooden frame with wide metal mesh inset within the frame. Two of these frames are then bolted together with layers of leaves, grass or similar filling pressed firmly between the two halves and then the structure is suspended either horizontally or vertically and small treats are hidden within the grassy filling to be searched for and manipulated out from between the mesh. The suspended frames are generally swinging freely at the same time. A great way to imitate foraging techniques. Another option is to have one piece with mesh inlaid and one piece with a solid bottom half, again bolted together like a flower press. These are for use horizontally as an alternative and you will see several primates clustered around the edges of this swinging contraption, busy foraging for goodies in the middle, like a knit and natter circle or suchlike. It sounded simple enough, cutting the wood to size, but I have never come across such hard wood in my life. It is a hardwood (which is actually classed as Vulnerable and therefore needing protection from extinction, the same as differing species of animal or rare plants, but we were using old recycled bits so were not impacting on the eco-system). The specific hardwood we were using is called Belian, but its also known as Ironwood, and I can tell you, it certainly lives up to its name, it took forever to saw through!!

As a bonus task I have now taken on the responsibility of the daily 3 o'clock feed for the pig-tailed macaques and Emily the gibbon, up on the hill, giving me a chance to stretch my legs and visit my favourite residents at the centre, whilst also giving my arms and hands a rest from sawing!

On my return I decided to pop in to visit Aman, the centres only adult male Orangutan, at that time. We have 6 orangs in total with the girls being Chiam and her baby daughter Mamu, Ghanti, Doris and Ting San. Aman is around 19 years old (Orangs can live to around 35-45 years in the wild but up to 60 years old in captivity) with a fully grown male averaging around 85kg in weight with an 8' arm span. He is a unique lad as, on May 16th of this year, 2007, he underwent groundbreaking cataract surgery, to remove cataracts from both eyes. The operation took around 2½ hours and was performed by a South African animal ophthalmologist called Izak Venter. This operation had never been performed on an orangutan before but was completely successful, giving Aman the ability to see again. He had been suffering from decreasing eyesight for the past 7 years. Apparently rescued from a Sarawak market in 1989 he had spent his life in Semanggoh Wildlife Park, before transferring to

Matang in 2000. Aman is a majestic chap and you get a special feeling when you are close to him, as if he could almost talk to you. During that special impromptu time in the Orangutan house he approached the bars of his bedroom enclosure and gently and slowly placed his finger through the bars, looked towards me, inviting me to join him for a moment. They say Orangutans do not have facial expression, I beg to differ. It was just a mutual finger stroke, a simple touch to connect and say 'Hi', but it meant more than mere words. A mutual understanding of his situation there, a shared moment which I cherished and did not take lightly. I must say at this point that any interaction was only at the initiation from the animals themselves. They have the freedom of their enclosures and choice of whether to interact with you through the bars or not. If they choose to invite me to I am more than happy but will not impose my own selfish desires on them. Doris was also interested in interacting with me through the window in her door, wanting to help me sweep the last little bits along the corridor edge. Any interaction with the orangs, and most animals here, has since been stopped. Only permanent members of staff, who have a long-term relationship and understanding of these individuals, will have any physical contact. Still, what a wonderful experience I had, to share these moments on a purely one-to-one basis. I did remind myself of the WOX mantra that made me want to choose this project – 'before you touch any animal think, is it for their benefit, or yours'. A simple phrase, but one I have never forgotten and will always endeavour to follow.

Incidentally, the name Orangutan comes from two Malaysian/Indonesian words - '*Orang*' meaning 'person' or 'man'and '*Utan*' deriving from 'hutan' meaning 'forest'. Therefore Orangutan is 'person of the forest' or 'man of the forest'. *'Mawas'* is also a Malay word for 'ape' or 'orangutan'.

My evening was a quiet relaxed one, reflecting on the days events, then reading some of a book I had brought with me called "Into the Heart of Borneo" by Redmond O'Hanlon. I learned about 2 fascinating birds in this book. Firstly, according to O'Hanlon, there is an owl near Mount Tiban in Borneo which is about the size of your thumb, and goes 'Poop-te-poop-poop'. Its called *Glucidium borneoense.* The second is a tiny hawk, *Microhierax* which apparently lays a large white egg, about as big as itself. These birds are cited as being smaller than some of the butterflies here. It seems then that the birds are tiny but the bugs are massive! After reading for a little while I spent some time chatting with the other volunteers before then attempting to cook myself a sumptuous meal. I may actually be improving on the cuisine front as my meal tonight was much better, even though it was cheating being a rather European affair of pasta twists with tinned tuna and sweetcorn. Maybe if I had been vegan then, as I am now, I would have faired much better!

Another day dawned at MWC (my eighth day) and my first duty was the Sambar Deer (Tim and Simon). Sambar deer are quite a large breed, with dark, long course hair and a relatively long, usually black, tail. Males have antlers with 3 tines on each. The morning duties always consisted of working in teams of two, for safety reasons and to have someone to enjoy the work with. Having found a big branch of tasty browse, myself and my teammate for the morning held it up in different positions and heights, to see how we thought they would like it best, going by the interest shown in our activities by the two deer themselves. We eventually settled on the perfect spot where they could enjoy munching on it happily. They absolutely loved it and were both spotted later in the day laying under it for shade. Double enrichment bonus.

After initial morning duties the rest of the day was all hands on deck. Armed with two tubs of paint we all set about the huge task of painting the walls of the new Sun Bear enclosure. We really struggled in the heat and were totally exhausted by lunchtime, but we used up all the paint so felt very proud of ourselves. This enclosure had just recently been built, after Heather and her husband spent a great deal of time fundraising, single-handedly, in order to free the 4 Bears currently stuck in the Quarantine 'cells'. An amazing achievement and hopefully Heather will be able to see the initial release of the bears into this enclosure before returning to the UK. For these bears to be able to see the sky, experience the earth and grass beneath their feet and feel the Sun on their faces is an unimaginable dream for them, having spent most of their lives in 2 pretty small square enclosures. These were tiled on the floor and walls, with bars stretching across the front. They had one raised wooden platform to sleep on and a corrugated roof. The covered walkway in front of the quarantine cages was lit with fluorescent lights, which were permanently on day and night, for security purposes I was told. This meant the animals never saw the sky or the stars and never had the luxury of darkness in which to sleep and rest. They could not be moved from this cell for cleaning either, so must avoid the daily hose spray as best they can, whilst faeces, urine and food waste are sprayed away into outside drainage channels. After cleaning the floor is wet, cold and slippery under their feet. This is not what the centre wants for their bears. Quarantine areas are, as they suggest, merely temporary holding areas for use to assess and carry out health checks of animals when they first arrive, prior to release or mixing with current residents, to avoid bringing in any diseases. However, with no other secure enclosures within the park they have no alternative but to be held there until such a time as amazing people such as Heather come along, see what needs to be done, then return home to make that happen, through fundraising and personal donation. So, despite the hardship of painting 15' high solid concrete walls in the burning heat, to be a part of this imminent release programme makes it just so worth a little hardship. Whilst we were doing this Heather was busy making up replica termite mounds for the bears and Ting San actually chipped in and came up trumps when they were out in forest school. She found a live termite mound and, before she could be stopped but again, showing good natural instincts, promptly broke off a large chunk. This was brought back and split between the 4 quarantine bears. They were absolutely ecstatic, especially the 2 named Corinne and Situ. Who could ever deny these little bears such a huge reward?

The Sun continued to beat down after lunch, although we did get a sudden downfall of rain. It is always a definite DOWNfall, there is no slanting of rain whatsoever as there is no breeze here and the raindrops are big and heavy! We had felt very relieved when the paint had been used up but, unfortunately, more paint was found, so we returned to painting the bear walls once the rain had subsided. Looking up at a 15' wall into direct sunlight makes for hard going painting, albeit with a roller, when sweat is running into your eyes and blinding you. Luckily, I had a brief respite at 3 o'clock when I had the chance to have a stroll and a stretch in the shade, to do my new duties of afternoon feeds up on the hill.

As our work day finished Leanne, Jenny and myself headed straight to the river to cool off. Sitting amongst the boulders, shoulders under the 'rapids', giving me a lovely gentle and cooling massage was, I must admit, total and utter bliss. Heather is out again this evening and I'm so weary so have decided on an early night again. I feel bad about it but I am not up to socialising as, apart from feeling weary I may be tempted to smoke again. Most of the other volunteers smoke and it would be so easy to just slip back into it but I really don't want to, having worked so hard to be free of the habit for 18 months. I thought it best to steer well clear! Since arriving here I had not experienced any trouble with mosquitos biting me so had not bothered with putting my mosquito net up over my bed, particularly as the walls and ceilings are so hard. Trying to get the hooks in is nigh on impossible. However, I am now starting to get bitten a fair bit and decided to have another go at putting it up. I struggled briefly but had to concede and gave up trying, deciding to just lay the net across the bed to see if that did the trick! I don't know what these houses are constructed of but they are solidly built that's for sure.

It was around 2am when I was awoken by the beeps of a text message coming through on my phone. This is the 3rd time this has happened to me. It is lovely to hear from people back home but they do seem to forget the time difference! I woke again around 4 am and my neck and jawline were itching like crazy. I had to get up, scrub my face with soap and cold water and but the air-con fan on.

The itching subsided after a while but drove me absolutely potty. In hindsight it was probably the insect repellent impregnated into my mosquito-net (generally Permethrin or Deltamethrin) that had touched my skin and caused an irritation. Not such a good idea draping it over my bed then – I'd better hang it up properly. To add to my woes, I also find myself with a very gunky and waxy left ear today. What a poor little morsel am I!

With the rash still on my neck and face all of the following day, Deb very kindly gave me some antihistamine tablets to try to clear it up. Painting the bear enclosure walls again in the searing heat of the morning probably didn't help my affliction but the afternoon gave some respite with some cloud cover and a trip into Matang Jaya to do a spot of shopping. This was a good opportunity to phone home as I get a good Digi (phonecard) signal here. It was lovely to hear the voices of Mum & Dad and my partner Ginj. Chatting away happily whilst squatting on an empty pallet outside the shopping plaza, I watched the pink sky suddenly come alive with forked lightening. The air was still so warm though, reminding me I was in a totally different world to the folks I was chatting to back home. I also found two alternative kinds of phone cards which should allow me to phone home cheaper and be able to text from the my home back in Matang too, which means I can keep in touch more regularly.

Of course, this was 12 years ago, in 2007, and things have changed. Now we would have no trouble chatting on Facetime or WhatsApp with our own phones Sim card still in place. No need to buy local Sim cards any more. Friends and family can now not only hear you on the phone but see you and see where you are, experiencing snapshots of your adventure with you, and generally free of charge to boot. Incredible progress.

My ears are getting worse quite rapidly and by the next day were really bad. Both now full of wax and pretty much completely deaf in the left ear. Horrible, annoying feeling, which I can remember well as I am currently going through the same situation as I am writing now. It seems this condition plagues me once every 5 years or so!

Heather and Deb went to Kuching so kindly sought out some ear drops for me and Sandra also came over with some ear drops she had brought out with her. I am here with such lovely people who all pull together to overcome any problem one of us may face. A perfect team. All I know is I have got to get rid of this predicament as soon as possible.

On a good note, Heather and Deb also managed to get hold of some bacon (from Ting & Tings shop I believe, which is based in Kuching and sells overseas delights in the food and alcohol line, to cater to the yearnings of homesick travellers and ex-pats)! Perfect, the bacon will go down a treat with the cheesy beans I found in the shop yesterday. Home from home. Its funny how you can love the cuisine of any country you live in and are happy to eat local dishes but, come across any silly thing from back home and you just crave it for no real reason! You may not even eat it normally but when you see a little slice of home you just go all gooey and have to buy it to reconnect in some way.

I was working with the rest of the group that day, clearing the grass cuttings (scythed not mowed as mown grass is unsuitable as food) from Doris's enclosure and feeding them to the deer and other herbivore species for enrichment. We also came across some old wooden puzzle feeders in the storage areas and set about cleaning them up and coating them in wood preserver (safe for animals in these instances) to be used later. As I was returning from my scheduled lunchtime feeding and enrichment visit to the pig-tailed macaques, I happened to meet Caroline coming back from the forest with Ting San. Ting San decided she would take my hand and walk with me a little way, trying to convince me to take her around a trail where fruit trees are now coming alive. However, it's time for her lunch and ours, so she climbed into my arms as if she was happily accepting to go along with this schedule, before suddenly reaching out and securely attaching herself to a signpost with both hands, in her little toddler defiance! Of course, a toddler orang is a heck of a lot stronger than a human toddler so it took a fair bit of convincing, but we managed to eventually, somehow reassuring her that the trail would still be there after lunch and that a little rest in the shade of her bedroom was a better option at this moment in time.

The rest of the volunteer girls had started painting trees on the bear enclosure walls. Jenny was cutting up foam mattress and shaping to use as leaf stencils. I added my little suggestion of copying broccoli heads of differing sizes to simulate the effect of treetops along the upper canopy, not that I had seen any broccoli since I had been here!

Heather returned from her latest trip away from the centre, bringing 3 durian fruits back with her in the taxi (it was a 45 minute drive!) Mr Boon, our regular taxi man, is such a nice guy, and has come to know Heather very well during her frequent trips here, but still, I am amazed he allowed it. It is true - they absolutely reek. I kept moving them around different areas to try to keep the smell away from the house but, despite being a calm and sticky evening it still managed to waft its putrid rotting onion smell around. Disgusting. The keepers and animals will love them though.

We were all excited as Keith had told us that its 'Doris Day' tomorrow – a chance to go in and interact with Doris the Orangutan, if we want to. It's something she's used to as over the years she has become very humanised and seems to enjoy it. She has been introduced to the forest on soft release on several occasions but each time she has chosen to return under her own steam and ask to be let back in. I will go in with her if this is what Doris enjoys and hopefully I will be a good companion for her.

"The use of travelling is to regulate imagination with reality, and instead of thinking of how things may be, see them as they are"

Samuel Johnson

CHAPTER FIVE

"The traveller sees what he sees, the tourist sees what he has come to see"

Gilbert K Chesterton

What a great day. During the usual morning duties I got the chance to have a good grooming session with Boboy. He is only a youngster, eager for physical contact and comfort. I have formed a nice little bond and mutual respect with Boboy during the time I have been working here and also with his neighbour Matt who is a striking chap having 2 differently coloured eyes, the same as David Bowie. Both Boboy and Matt are Long Tailed Macaques, also known as Crab-eating Macaques. Malay words for them are *Kera* or *Beruk*. These primates can live to around 30 years old and weigh around 8.5kg (male) and 5.5kg (female). Their tails are longer than their bodies and they are excellent swimmers, which is something you don't really think of when you see monkeys. They can be found sleeping in trees, huddling together for warmth and comfort and their main diet is ripe fruit, supplemented with insects, leaves, eggs, clay, bark, seeds, flowers etc. They will also eat crabs, hence the name, as well as frogs, shrimps and octopus.

Sadly these macaques are considered a pest as they will raid crops and houses.

One line of thinking is to allow people visiting nature reserves to feed them, thus keeping them controlled within a certain area and preventing the need for them to forage elsewhere. The downside to this is that people tend to feed inappropriate food to the animals, causing them to become ill, weak and deficient in vital nutrients. It can also cause them to become overconfident with people and start to attack them to steal food from visitors whether offered or not. This can result in conflict and harm to both macaques and humans. Primates and humans share some diseases (Zoonotics) and therefore can transfer potentially fatal diseases to one another through injuries. I was told whilst there that the best way to scare away a macaque if it became too persistent was to mime pulling back a catapult with your hands. Apparently these are used to scare them away in certain areas! It is an ongoing conflict the more humans spread out and encroach on the habitat of wild animals worldwide.

Then, the time had come, time to go in with Doris the orangutan on a one-to-one. We all watched from the orangutan viewing platform whilst taking it in turns to head down and enter the world of Doris. I must say it gives you an idea of what animals feel like when they are being watched from above, whether friendly faces or not. The outside enclosure is very large with a massive climbing platform in the centre where Doris can climb to eye level with the visitors viewing platform the other side of the wall. Keith remained with Doris the whole time so he was able to let us in and out and ensure she was totally happy during the meetings and all was safe. Having many years of experience in close contact with great apes in different zoos, I knew Keith was an expert in these situations and trusted his judgement completely. He also kindly took our cameras as we entered, to ensure we had some lasting mementos of our very special experience. It was interesting to see that Doris behaved quite differently with each of us. She was very quiet and settled into having a gentle time with Deb, whereas she decided to take Leanne for random walks around the enclosure quite a bit! With me, it was a range of behaviours. Starting quietly then interacting and wrestling with me, giggling and rolling around as I tickled her. Then, as my time was drawing to an end, we had a quiet and quizzical time as she studied and watched me as I concentrated on tying together bits of grass and drawing outlines and pictures in the dirt with twigs and stones. She watched me very carefully and took it all in. Hopefully she enjoyed it as much as I did. You cannot begin to explain how it feels to be so intimate with another species, being their entertainment if you like, rather than the other way around. As I mentioned before, Doris is so comfortable here, she prefers to interact with humans than return to her forest home, at least for the moment.

For enrichment we filled the puzzle feeders with dry leaf litter and then hid small treats inside the leaves before giving to the macaques and the gibbons. That should keep them busy for quite a while, manipulating the leaves as they would in the wild to obtain small tasty berries and fruits. All seemed to absolutely love them and got foraging immediately. Whilst we were doing all this, Heather and Caroline had taken Ting San into the forest to video her with a whole durian fruit. Apparently she opened it up NO problem at all. Smart little girl. Excellent to see how many skills she already has, preparing her to live in the wild.

In the evening we were all in for a special treat. We had been invited for a meal out at Jambu Restaurant and Lounge in Kuching. This is a beautiful boutique restaurant, just outside the centre of Kuching. It is run by a guy from Newcastle and his local wife. The restaurant is situated in a 1920's colonial bungalow from the Raja Brooke era, with teak floors, high ceilings and coloured lanterns. The courtyard area had a beautiful water feature running around the garden, bringing the outside in and the inside out. We were made so welcome and the food was amazing. A really great, relaxing night. What an amazing day Friday, 19th October 2007 had turned out to be.

The following morning my experience here was to continue to delight. Being Saturday I was due to have a day off and had planned to go on the waterfall trail with Deb and Leanne. However, the centre was short staffed again, with only Keith on duty and Heather with Ting San so I decided to stay and lend a hand. Kevin, one of the pig-tailed macaque boys on the hill was giving me hugs and gently touching my legs through the bars when I went up to feed them. An amazing and special feeling which was totally unexpected and gentle, making me fall in love with these guys even more. What with this and my daily grooming from Boboy too – how privileged am I.

Pig-tailed macaques are larger than the long-tailed ones with males weighing up to around 14.5kg. Their tails are stubby and curled, like pigs' tails, hence the name, and they can live to around 25 years old. Roughly 75% of the diet is fruit based, supplemented with insects, seeds, leaves, dirt, fungus etc. They are also known to raid plantations for coconuts, papaya, corn, cassava etc, usually having one of the troop keep lookout. People actually capture them as babies, forcing them from their mothers, very often by actually killing the mother. They are then tied on a rope around their necks, and used to collect coconuts from the tops of trees to sell as an income.

Being vegan nowadays I use a lot of coconut products, such as coconut oil, but try to source brands that state no monkeys were used to gather the coconuts.

I had every intention of helping out to ease the burden of work from Keith and Heather but I can barely hear anything now, my ears have blocked up so much. Heather insisted that after work I should go to hospital and Keith agreed, driving us both into Kuching and dropping us right outside the hospital before returning back to his home. I wouldn't have had a clue what to do but Heather seemed totally aware of the system and looked after me with such an easy calm that I lost any stress and nerves. The Hospital was very good, albeit a bit bizarre in its methods. Upon arrival you are asked to explain your circumstances and the reason for your visit to a man stationed at a desk outside the hospital. He writes down the illness on a form and hands the form to you to take inside. You then take this form in to the main desk and explain your illness again, whilst paying RM50 (as a visitor to the country) and wait for triage. I was then questioned again, by the same man from the main desk, and he proceeded to examine my ears with a big household torch! Then I was told to move through to the next area and wait to see the Doctor. They did seem to find my name quite amusing for some reason, maybe they know about Florence Nightingale. Eventually, I was called in to see the Doctor, who was really nice and very good at English. It was so nice to notice then that all the Doctors, having ascertained that I was English, continued to talk to me, and one another, in English also. Even the next patient nearby, a schoolteacher, reverted to English. So polite and friendly of them all to do that and help put me at ease. It meant such a lot and does make you realise how poorly we fair across the world when it comes to making an effort to learn other languages properly. Everyone was so very polite here. It turns out I have compacted ear wax, which can occur sometimes after long haul flights, exacerbated by working in hot and humid conditions. I was prescribed some ear drops, to soften the wax, and told to return to the hospital to get my ears syringed in 5 days time. The final part of the visit involved walking through the hospital to the in-house pharmacy. I was handed a ticket number at the first window and then, when my number came up I then had to present myself at the second window, where the medications were given out, at no extra charge. I had a giggle to myself as it felt like I was in Argos with my little ticket number waiting for it to come up like some very short game of Bingo, where you always win, as long as you sit and wait long enough.

On leaving the hospital, Heather and I got a taxi into Kuching Centre and went for a meal in a restaurant overlooking the waterfront that I had already come to love during my short time here. I plumped for a Cheeseburger with mushrooms and a Cappucino milkshake. The food and the setting were both stunning. It was actually a huge meal which equated to be only around £3.75. At the end of the evening we caught a Taxi back to MWC and to top off a beautiful evening were privileged to see fireflys as we were walking back to the bilik. Who needs glow sticks and fireworks, you can't beat the beauty and intricacy of nature. Heather is so nice, I discovered she had actually given up an invitation to attend a Saturday night beach party for a hotel opening night, just to sort me out and keep me company.

Heather and I worked the following day too, to give Keith and Caroline a very rare day off together. As the others are all at Singgahsana for the weekend (England playing rugby final tonight), Heather gave me a real treat and let me go and sit with her and Ting San in the forest for a bit. How amazing to see that little orange bundle climb and swing amongst the trees. I am so honoured as I would never have had that experience at any rescue project and only got to do this as I stayed back with my ear infection. Funny how things work out. As we sat on one of the forest platforms I spotted a pure white, what seemed to be, fluffy leech. I had never seen or heard of a fluffy one before and have never found it in any books since (so maybe it wasn't a leech but something else). Totally fascinating watching it dance and stand upright on the end of its tail as it stretched up to try to touch my finger hovering just above its head, smelling the presence of skin and wanting to suck my blood. Heather also pointed out that the vines (Liana I assume) only grow around fig trees here, yet you cannot find figs to buy, despite the abundance of fig trees. She also showed me a Ratan plant, one of the many palm species. Apparently the fruit grows at ground level in the centre, around June time. The fruit is extremely citrus and sour and the stems have protective prickles (which they use to climb up, and attach to, host trees). If the prickles are removed or blunted by rubbing on a tree, the leaf stems inside are then eaten by Orangutans too. We all know that handicrafts and furniture are fashioned from rattan stems so it is nice to see their origins.

The following day I reached a low point with my ears and lack of hearing. My phone card loading skills were poor to say the least, having to follow recorded messages to install each time so phoning home was not happening as much as I intended. To top it all I was feeling totally exhausted in the heat. Not feeling too good when I woke up, I decided to stay off work for the morning and laid in until 11.30. I ended up getting bitten to hell all over my legs but, still, I did feel heaps better, although still deaf! To help my motivation, Deb booked for us to have a traditional Bornean tattoo on Saturday – wicked. We had wanted to do this for some time and looked into reputable local tattooists. Ernesto Kalum, of Borneo Headhunter Tattoo Studio, is based in Kuching but can often be seen travelling worldwide with tattoo conventions. He came highly recommended by several people and, in my opinion, Ernesto is one of the best in the business. He is an Iban, using traditional methods and personalised designs. Very exciting.

I worked the afternoon OK and returned to the Bilik where I said farewell to Heather. She was off to Sipidan for a diving and snorkelling break until Thursday night so I was home alone once more. Aqil came to visit and check to see if I was OK or if I needed anything. Then Gavin, co-founder of WOX and visiting for a few days, also came over for the same reason. All such nice people here.

When I was growing up, one of my favourite quick meals was tinned tomatoes and sausage meat (or bacon), mopped up with slices of bread. Its funny when you travel how you fancy the funniest things. Since this project I have done others around the world and my 'go to' yearning always seems to be tomatoes for some reason. Anyway, I had found some bacon so set to and decided to recreate this simple, tasty dish. Surely I couldn't go wrong with this meal! I fried up the bacon then opened the tin of tomatoes and promptly tipped into the frying pan with the bacon to heat through. Big mistake. Turned out to be a big tin of tomato puree. Doh! I had nothing else and was hungry so I scraped what I could off the bacon and ate some, but it wasn't good! However, what I could salvage of this hearty meal was enough to set me up well for my evening chores of changing my sheets, doing a load of washing and putting up my mosquito net properly. I am sick of being bitten now and don't want dengue fever to go with my deaf ears and chin rash!

After the chores I successfully reloaded my phone so was able to phone home for a good chat. Before coming abroad I had hidden presents around the house for my partner, little treats to help pass the time for her while I was away. It was time for a clue to where present number 2 was hidden (a Playstation game). As we chatted my right ear was popping away merrily so hopefully the ear drops are starting to work.

My right ear continued to pop the next day, and actually cleared for an hour or so in the evening, giving me a little glimmer of half decent conversation and a sign of returning to normality. The main job of the day was to clean out, paint and re-rope Chiam, Mamu and Ghanti's outdoor enclosure. Now, being an animal keeper, I am obsessed with rope and I must say the rope you can get here is fantastic. Stuff we could only dream of back home as it is just so expensive there. The girls had to be confined to their inside quarters whilst we were working but it will be well worth it for them. They watched us with interest most of the time but Chiam was bullying Ghanti horribly, making her squeal. The sounds were similar to a pig snorting and squeaking, but really not nice to witness. Poor Ghanti. The heavens opened the second half of the afternoon and didn't stop again until around 6pm. We got home to find we had a power cut at the house again. This had happened yesterday and a few days ago too. We found the main switch under our neighbour's house, after checking with Leah who showed us where it was, and all came back on OK again. At least we now know how to turn the power back on if it happens again. I decided to boil up the kettle for a warm 'mandi' this evening. It's the first time we've all felt a bit chilly since arriving, but when you get caught in rain for any length of time, it does penetrate and cool you down a little too much! Hopefully this has cleared the air a bit and reduced the humidity as it was a really heavy storm, so should have done the trick if the weather back home is anything to go by.

Leanne and Deb invited me over for dinner this evening which was great. Leanne cooked pasta in spicy tomato and bacon sauce and Deb supplied the beer. It was a lovely evening. They have a sweet cat, called Wanda, who is tortoiseshell and unlike all the others. The rest of the cats around here are a tabby Siamese cross and all part of the same family – the Daisy clan. We have Daisy, Baby Daisy and Baby Daisy's babies! (or BDB's). Cats here are generally small and born with only a short stumpy and/or kinked tail. Apparently only around 20% of cats have a complete tail, 20% have no tail at all, and the rest have the stumpy kinked tails. Their are many stories of why this is but it appears to be a genetic mutation which has remained over many years.

Not great for balance, communication or keeping insects at bay but the cats seem to do just fine.

We did awaken the following morning to a day that was a bit cooler following the storm but we were still sweating buckets nonetheless. Keith and Caroline have been running Matang for 2 years now but their time will soon be coming to an end, handing the reins over to Tim and Aqil to carry on the good work. This must be so hard for them as any placement caring for wildlife grabs you hard emotionally from the outset, no matter where in the world you happen to be. How they both must feel leaving after building the place up for so long I cannot even begin to imagine. They are both exhausted, showing testament to how much energy they have invested in Matang. As an animal keeper I was absolutely thrilled today as Keith showed us how to splice rope ends together, a great thing to learn, especially as their rope is so huge and thick. Did I mention I absolutely love rope?! Here is the method we learned:

1) Bend rope end back on itself and secure with tape or metal collar (adjustable).
2) Get length of securing twine (approx 8' length). Make a loop and hold in place up the shaft of the rope with your thumb. Wrap the twine around both pieces of rope shaft several times (10-12 approx), pulling as tight as possible each time.
3) Pass the end of the twine through the loop you had made and pull the tail piece. This will take the loop down behind the wrapped twine in a knot-type hold.
4) Use a Fyd (specialist splicing tool) to separate the tied rope above and beneath the binding to enable

the passing of the twine through the middle of the two pieces of rope lengthways. Do this twice, then tie off with a knot, using the remaining end and tail piece. An illustration of the finished article can be found in the photograph section of the book.

It all looks very neat and is extremely secure without the need for harmful and unnatural fixings such as metal, which can be sharp and rust over time.

Those steps up to the Sun Bears are still killing my legs and lungs when I do my enrichment rounds, so I don't think my fitness has improved yet. It has been 2 weeks! The main enrichment tasks today included drilling holes in logs for future use for many different animals. The holes can be filled with honey for the bears to lick out, or other substances for other animals to lick. Also various types of food treats, such as raisins, berries, small chopped pieces of vegetable, mashed banana can be manipulated out of the holes with deft little primate fingers. This type of enrichment draws on them naturally acquiring food from small crevices and takes a lot of time to achieve so keeping their brains active without piling on the weight because only a small amount of food will be gained from the exercise. We also installed a suspended bucket in the enclosure of Theresa the gibbon. This could be used to fill with grasses, leaves, treats etc and she absolutely loved it, promptly spending many a time sitting in it, like a nest of some kind! Whilst Deb and I were doing the splicing and the enrichment, the rest of the girls worked hard on finishing the painting of Chiam and Ghanti's outdoor enclosure. They are real painting demons, determined to do it all and not interested in any other jobs (Sandra, Chris and Jenny). They are doing a cracking job painting pictures in the

Bear enclosure too. Happy to leave them to it. Good news too – my right ear had sound 99% of today – such a relief. I will be getting them syringed tomorrow and all will be well again hopefully. Can't wait for full service to be resumed!

My attempts at cooking that evening failed dismally again! I cooked a portion of pasta then added some of the tomato puree (from my attempt 2 days ago), an Italian stock cube, a tin of whole mushrooms and some cheese. The mushrooms tasted like slimy dirt and the cheese was all stringy and gooey, sticking around my gums and teeth. Not nice at all!

Once dinner was dispensed with my endless stream of filthy, sweaty clothes needed to be done yet again but once finished I rewarded myself by relaxing on the verandah and reading until it was time to call it a night.

I later learned that the day we arrived at Matang, a couple of Pig-tailed Macaques, both of which were very young, had been brought in together. As the keepers were trying to put them into a quarantine cage one of the two gave them the slip, managing to wriggle free, and ran off. Finding itself now alone, the other one was absolutely terrified so it was decided that it was better to release them both together so they had more chance of survival with companionship, rather than keep one back alone. The intention was an early release, once a health check had been carried out on them both anyway, so it would have been pointless to health check one and then release it with the other, who was unchecked. I watched as one of them appeared near my bilik foraging for breakfast on the 17th morning of their escape. I didn't spot the other one and worried that it may not have survived but hopefully it was also nearby and they will both be OK and enjoy a better life than the captive ones. If they are sensible they will stick together, close to the centre for a while where there is an opportunity of plenty of food, whilst they get their bearings and learn where the fruiting trees are, moving away into the wild as they become confident.

Apparently there is going to be an inspection on Monday so it was absolutely great to arrive at the centre for work that morning to see that the keepers had been in and cleaned Emily and the macaques enclosures out properly. What a treat for them all. I am going to train Emily to eventually go in the smaller inner caged area of her enclosure for her afternoon feed so we can then aim to shut her in, stress-free, in the future, whilst we can then enter and put some furnishings in her enclosure and make it super smart and suitable for a gibbon. At the moment it is only local, permanent keepers who will ever go in with the animals. However, this is not ideal or safe on either side, so for the keepers to be able to go in and clean daily in the future and add enrichment will be a massive step forward.

Gavin invited us all to join him on a spur of the moment forest trek. It was a bit short notice though and we didn't feel it was fair on Keith and Caroline for us all to suddenly disappear, so Deb, Leanne and I decided to stay and carry on working whilst Gavin took the others to Kubah. He took them to a fantastic waterfall apparently, so I would have been so miffed if I had gone. I absolutely love waterfalls and to not be able to go in, due to my ears, would have been extremely frustrating.

Talking of ears, today was the day though and so it was off to Kuching at 3.30pm to have them syringed, before doing the weekly shop on the way back. Dr Chang couldn't do my ears as we thought he would, but instead sent us to Timberland Medical Centre and the Ear, Nose & Throat specialist. Eventually, my wait was over and by 5.30 I could hear again. Tons of disgusting wax washed out from within my ears into the waiting bowl below. Yuk! How happy am I – wahoo, the world is back in glorious surround sound.

We picked up the others who, after finishing their trek, had been to Ting & Ting supermarket for some bacon and then on to Singghasana to use the internet. Gavin then treated us to a surprise trip to one of the most memorable meals I have ever had. It was at a place called "L L Banana Leaf" and situated in Rubber Road, Kuching. This is a South Indian food cafe, where your meal is served on a banana leaf, if you ask for it. All little side dishes were laid out in small piles across the top of the leaf (cucumber, pineapple chutney, fish, etc) then rice was placed on the main central part of the leaf and your meat dish and dahl dish were placed on the side. It was all washed down with 2 glasses of fresh mango lasse – all for about £1.50. Oh and 2 poppadoms as well. Wonderful, wonderful meal.

Shopping at Choice Ria supermarket finished our trip, returning home around 9pm when we boiled up a dozen eggs, ready for enrichment tomorrow. Before bed I phoned Ginj and Mum & Dad. All the family are good and Mum informed me she had made her Christmas cake today. There's me, 10pm, sweltering on my verandah in shorts and T-shirt, little cat for company, and there's my mum, in the UK, making Christmas cake. It all seems very odd.

The usual wake up call here, apart from the animals, is the 5.30am school bus for Jemma, the little girl in the bilik opposite Heather and I. Its still pitch black poor little mite but at least they do get back home around 1pm and have the rest of the day to play or escape the heat. Also this morning, Heather returned from her visit to Sipidan. Her back is badly sunburnt from snorkelling so I tried to ease it by slapping on Aloe Vera throughout the day.

We had the pleasure of having to look after 5 volunteers from another project, called Orangutan Experience I think, and they were known as Orangutarians! Their particular experience and trip to Borneo is a 2 week jolly, visiting the forest on a general trek before heading to Semenggoh Wildlife Centre, Bako National Park and us here at Matang Wildlife centre, looking for orangutans specifically. The group all seemed really nice, except one mouthy, highly opinionated one who managed to really wind us all up. He wanted to put Corinne (Sun Bear) in a crate and totally transform her area in an hour, to make his holiday and her life complete. What does he think we're all doing here, oh yes, apart from actually grafting, getting involved physically, on the ground, with the animals. He thinks he's Lawrence Llewellyn-Bowen on animal changing rooms I think. I introduced them all to Behavioural Enrichment and then managed to avoid them for the rest of the afternoon. It was a shame really because the others, especially his girlfriend, were really nice and wanted to learn more and help out, rather than offer endless unfounded opinions.

In the evening we arranged a get together with this group, our group and the local families, organising a BBQ for them down by the river. All our girls made pasta dishes, Heather and I did salad, potatoes and burgers, and we also had corn on the cob, sausage, chicken, bananas with chocolate, tuak (locally made rice wine), beer and vodka. James, the permanent animal manager at Matang who lives opposite Heather and I with his family, manned the BBQ with his trusty accomplice Aqil. It appears that BBQs are a man thing the world over! The food was fantastic and the setting by the river was really nice, although the circular wooden, open sided structure that had a central table and benches around the edges absolutely stunk of cat wee in some areas! Some of our cats came along and joined us at the BBQ, showing us this is a regular hot spot for them and they are quite at home here. Hence the smell!

Whilst at the BBQ we also informed James of our apparent ghost, Martin. Heather was telling me she has had him sitting on her bed and ruffling her hair when staying here alone. I mentioned I kept hearing movements and the sink sponge keeps falling on the floor. Our neighbour says he heard Martin coughing when the house was empty and Leah, James' wife, has apparently had him at her house too. He lived in our bilik with his wife and children, but died of TB earlier this year – June I think.

Anyway, James very kindly said he would come and perform an exorcism for us tomorrow. I stayed on at the BBQ site with Deb, Jenny, Aqil and Gill until the last candle went out then headed back home, only to find James had been and performed the exorcism already. Heather was in her pyjamas when he came round, finding time to get onto it straight away rather than risk any further visitations during the night. It was apparently a very traditional ceremony which entailed nailing pieces of black cloth to our front door, back door and both bedroom doors. Each piece of cloth had nails pushed through with the sharp ends pointing outwards. He then went around talking to 'Martin', asking him to leave, whilst sprinkling holy water and spitting Ginger around all the rooms. Apparently the black cloth stops the spirit seeing its way in, but if it does get through then the nails will hurt its feet. I didn't get to learn the reason for the spitting of ginger and its significance sadly. Very good of him to do this and I must say I never heard mention of any more visitations from Martin after that.

Later in the evening, sitting on the verandah, we noticed both of the escaped macaques together on the roof next door. It was good to see they were both together and seemed to be doing OK, but the larger one, a female that had been named Sandy, seems to have a broken left wrist. We informed James and Keith, but were told there isn't really much we can do without causing huge stress and problems for them. Trying to catch both again, put them in a cage and try to treat Sandy would be a very difficult task. It is best to try to monitor and keep an eye on them both, to ensure she copes well enough as it heals. At least by not trying to catch them, they should stay close by the houses, making monitoring them a lot easier. The smaller of the two is a male, called John Travolta apparently! Now I see the reason for Sandy getting her name – a nod to the film "Grease".

The following morning, Heather and I were providing breakfast for the Orangutarians, or the 'meaningfuls' as we had now tagged them. This meant that, although it was our day off, we actually needed to be up earlier than usual in order to cook for them. One of the cats had had diarrhoea on one of the dining chairs so Heather put it at the head of the table, thinking the gobby one would probably opt to sit there – we did, however, bottle out at the last minute though and just giggled to ourselves at the thought. And yes, he did walk in and immediately take his seat, at the head of the table!

Once they had finished breakfast, we cleared up and Heather, Deb and I headed into Kuching to have our traditional tattoos at Borneo Headhunters (Ernesto and Robin). What an experience – it was expensive but definitely worth it and a highlight of my life, up there with the sweat lodge I had been extremely privileged to be invited to during my travels across North America a few years ago. We approached the little red front door at 47 Wayang Street, Kuching, rang the bell and waited. We heard footsteps from inside and Robin, Ernesto's assistant, opened the door and welcomed us in, with a lovely warm smile. Shoes off, we headed up the steep, narrow staircase to the first floor where we met Ernesto himself, quietly singing and playing his acoustic guitar as he smoked a cigarette. Looking around the studio I noticed the walls of one half of the room were painted white, with framed photographs of previous customers. This half of the room had a chair for general tattooing, using a tattoo gun and for piercings. The back half of the room, where the traditional tattooing takes place, had the walls covered by lengths of bamboo, with fishing baskets and other ornaments hanging from them.

We all wanted to experience the traditional method, where Ernesto would use needles bound onto bamboo shafts and a leather bound mallet. It is similar to the idea of a sculptor using a hammer and chisel to fashion an intricate carving on a piece of stone or wood. The ink is sunk into the skin using quick downward taps. This method does not cause damage to the skin, whereas as an electric tattoo gun would as it scratches the surface of the skin. This also means the design is impregnated deeper and more concentrated so it will last longer, with better definition and no fading or blurring as the tattoo ages.

Ernesto was such a relaxed and gentle man, instantly putting us at ease whilst we chatted to him and discussed what designs we would like. He was happy to either use one of his previous designs or create one specifically for us. For mine he had designed a macaque on a tree of life, signifying my work here with the macaques, one of my favourite primates anyway, and the tree of life being a special symbol for me throughout life, as well as representing my feeling of belonging, here in the rainforests of Borneo. When my turn came, Ernesto asked me to lay on the bamboo mat on the wooden floor and relax. He settled cross legged beside me on the left, with Robin seated on the floor to my right. Robin would hold the skin taut as Ernesto set to work, tapping away at the design he had copied onto my left shoulder. I couldn't believe the speed at which his hands moved. He could have sent a whole short novel on a morse code machine whilst bringing my design to life. The procedure took a while, and Ernesto would stop a couple of times to stretch, have a cigarette and a strum on his guitar, before continuing. The tattoo procedure itself didn't hurt at all. I was surprised. Tattoo guns can be uncomfortable and irritating because they are scratching the skin but the traditional method is a meditational experience which you actually do not want to end. It could easily become addictive and I was already planning a return visit as my own session sadly came to an end. We spent the whole afternoon there with the guys, just chilling and chatting until all 3 of us had our new pieces of art. Totally amazing and special experience. I did promptly book in for another tattoo, after looking through Ernesto's books of designs and falling in love with one in particular. I didn't know why, but it just drew me in. I loved it, a traditional Iban design that had been built upon and personalised by Ernesto. This one would be taking pride of place on my right ankle. Thanking the guys for a wonderful afternoon, we left and headed back to Matang, with just enough time to get ready for our evening at the longhouse or *Rumah Panjai (Rumah* = house, *Panjai* = long).

Once a month, the keepers and their families open up their homes in their nearby village, where they spend their days off. This is their true family homes away from Matang. This evenings invitation had come from Umar, the main Orangutan keeper at Matang, and his wife. Each invitation includes all food, drink and entertainment, music and free-flowing home-made tuak.

The village was not far from the centre at all and everyone came out to greet us, many children running around excitedly, some peeping shyly around doorframes and through window openings. Teenagers, like any teenagers anywhere, huddled in groups looking slightly uncomfortable, peering from the shadows and whispering together. The Longhouse itself was not what I expected at all, being a long block of 27 doors in a wide, straight, polished concrete corridor with fluorescent lights overhead. There was a family behind each door, similar to one level of a block of flats in the

UK. The Government had moved most people from traditional wooden longhouses now, into places such as this which are actually much more comfortable and homely. Traditional longhouses, I was told, were very gloomy and poor to actually live in.

After initial introductions we were then welcomed in to eat with Umar. The women and children of his family did not join us, they would eat once we had finished. Lots of plates and dishes, full of food, were laid out on bamboo mats – tofu, chicken, fish, rice, vegetables and sauces, all washed down with squash. We settled down around the food on the floor, like a picnic, and tucked in to this lovely banquet. Sacks of freshly harvested rice were stacked against one wall, one basic dressing table and lino on the floor were the main fixtures and fittings of this home. The whole community comes together though, as one big family and you can see the closeness and contentment. Kids were playing on bikes up and down the concrete corridor as we left Umar's house, allowing the women and children to clear away our dishes and eat themselves. James was in charge of the Tuak then and ensured our glasses were always full. As the rice wine flowed the dancing and music began. A young girl appeared and performed 'The dance of the hornbill' in traditional costume for us – it was just so elegant and beautiful. We were totally captivated and wondered what all the intricate movements of body and limbs and fingers represented. The costume consisted of a *pua kumba* which is a traditional ceremonial textile covering the shoulders like a small poncho and ornamented with an edging of colourful pompoms.

Weaving on a backstrap loom is an Iban craft which women master and gain high social status through as it is so complex, depicting animals, goddesses and geometric designs. Our dancers' was mainly yellow and white, with red and blue designs and finished off with pink pompoms. Along with the *pua kumba* the dancer also wears an elaborate silver head-dress and an overskirt made from silver coins joined together, like chainmail. You can see the importance and symbolism of all these pieces of the costume and feel the pride of the wearer as she dances.

Seated on the floor along the back wall, some of the women were accompanying the dancing with an array of traditional tribal instruments called *bebendai* (medium sized gongs), *dedumba* (drums) and smaller gongs or *engkurumong* laid on the floor in front of them. These gongs are circular brass instruments of differing diameters, mounted horizontally onto wooden frames using rope.

The Dance of the Hornbill is one of the major dances at important ceremonies, the Rhinoceros Hornbill in particular being an important cultural symbol, with Borneo being known as "The Land Of The Hornbills". The Rhinoceros Hornbill can be seen on the official Crest of Sarawak. There are, I believe, 8 species of hornbill in Borneo with the rhinoceros being one of the 2 largest birds. It has an upturned horn or 'casque' above its bill, making it look like a rhinoceros (hence the name). This casque is hollow and so amplifies the call of the bird.

After the Hornbill dance was completed and we had a few minutes to catch our breath and chat about the dance, it was our turn to entertain by trying to copy the intricate, graceful moves of the young girl from earlier.

Of course we were all totally hopeless and everyone had a great laugh at our expense, us included. It was the least we could do for such a warm welcome, great food and stunning traditional show. Once our efforts had mercifully finished the ghetto blaster was switched on for a more western style of music. All the kids and the young girls were up dancing and now it was their turn to copy our western dance moves and styles, giggling happily.

The boys stayed away, peeping through the windows occasionally, as is tradition with all boys around the world! Sweet black coffee came round, followed by more Tuak and the whole evening was a lot of fun.

The only uncomfortable part of our visit was when I needed to visit the toilet. I was directed to a Malaysian style toilet at the back of the kitchen, which was a cubicle housing a ceramic hole in the otherwise tiled floor. There was no light and no lock on the door, plus the floor was wet. I tried squatting but just couldn't relax so ended up just holding it in for the rest of the evening. The fact that it was in the kitchen and I could hear everyone outside the door, washing up and chatting, whilst I tried to hold the door in the pitch black and squat just wasn't conducive to having a wee. Thank goodness that's all I needed to do!

Traditional toilets will have either a bucket of water and a scoop to clean yourself with afterwards, or a section of hosepipe connected to a tap for the same purpose, rather than using toilet paper, which cannot be processed in the sewage system here. Of course this means the floor is perpetually wet after being used. We think bidets are a relatively new and 'posh' addition to bathrooms but, like many modern 'inventions' these often stem from older traditional methods, so who is the most advanced? Certainly not us Westerners in many respects. If you do have a western toilet and toilet tissue is provided then you must put your soiled tissue in a waste paper bin by the side of the toilet and dispose of it separately, such as burning.

The evening came to a close and, as we left, everyone waved us goodbye. However, I then spotted a sad little girl stood waving alone, further down the street. Apparently she is excluded as her mum is unmarried. Even though half the women there were divorced. I wish I had known she was there earlier, we could maybe have done something with her. Such a sad little sight.

Khatulistiwa, Kuching

Singgahsana Lodge. Kuching(with multi-storey carpark behind)

Ting San

Accommodation at Matang

Splicing rope

Emily (Bornean Gibbon)

"Travel and change of place impart new vigour to the mind"

Seneca

CHAPTER SIX

"It is not down in any map, true places never are"
Herman Melville

The following day Heather and I worked so Keith and Caroline had some time out before Keith flies home tomorrow for a well earned break. This meant I could spend the whole morning in the forest with Heather and Ting San. Total magic and Ting San was very at ease and accepting of me. She has an amazing way of coming up close and staring deep into your eyes, as if she is staring right into your heart and your soul – so moving. She took my hand a few times as we walked along the forest paths, although rolling along is her usual preferred form of travel! I found a different type of flower frond and gave it to her. She studied it carefully, then pulled my hands gently to the ground as if to say 'show me again - where did that come from?' Wow!!

In the evening, once forest school was over for Ting San and all the other work was complete, Heather drove us to Matang Jaya so we could use the internet, emailing our news back home and catching up with messages and news from family and friends. Once finished we treated ourselves to a plate of Roti Canai, Heathers favourite meal, and Mango Lasse, my favourite drink. Roti Canai is a typical Malaysian dish of Roti (flat bread) with a chickpea dhal or chicken curry to dip it into, and is served for breakfast, lunch, dinner – any time of the day in fact. Mango Lasse is a drink made from fresh mango, milk, yoghurt and a bit of sugar, made into a smoothie. You can also add a bit of cardamom.

When we returned to our little village we decided to have a bit of a joke and so took 'the haunted sponge' over to Deb, Leanne and Gills bilik and wound them up! We were very convincing as they got all jittery and didn't really want it in the house!

Heather later gave me her Chinese monkey symbol charm, mounted on a leather lace as a necklace. This is the symbol she had chosen as her tattoo at Ernesto's so Heather no longer needed it in necklace form. I was originally also going to have this symbol as a tattoo but changed my mind, so I now have it as well as my chosen Tree of Life tattoo, which is a real bonus.

Phoning home before going to sleep Ginj told me that her beloved VW combi camper had been smashed into quite badly. Of course no one had left details or owned up to it, so she was a little upset by it. Ginj is a great artist, normally painting wonderful pictures of animals, but she told me she is painting a picture for me for when I return home, and it is not an animal one. I wonder what it is.

It is day 21 of our Bornean adventure and we are all really getting into the swing of things and understanding the animals and their differing needs and preferences. Enrichment wise, we started making a 'nest box' for Emily the gibbon, so she could shelter from the heavy rains when they come, especially once the hard rainy season begins. Normally, gibbons would sleep in the crook of a tree branch but at the moment there is nothing in Emily's enclosure to replicate that in any way nor has she any other means of shelter from the rain, so we shall address these issues bit by bit. Matty, the long-tailed macaque, was also a priority for me, he has a stereotypic behaviour of picking his arm hairs out so is developing a bald patch. When animals are not stimulated enough, either physically or mentally, in a captive setting they can become extremely stressed and depressed. Desperately seeking something to fill their time very often means turning attention inward, to themselves, as they have nothing to occupy them in their surroundings. In stark zoo settings you may well see animals pacing up and down the same, well worn path. They may walk in endless circles around their enclosure, or they may be seen sitting and rocking. We would be exactly the same if we had to live in one room, for our whole lives, with no furniture or forms of entertainment such as TV, phone, books, games etc. Matty is a smart boy, as all macaques are, so plenty of enrichment was given to him which kept him occupied for the majority of the day. Excellent.

There was a bit of friction between a couple of the volunteers. This is such a passionate and hard working group, who have all taken to the animals and want to work as hard as they can before the time comes when they must return home, which is only a few days away now, so motivation and drive is at its peak. Deb was busy digging holes for fence posts. As I mentioned earlier, she is an archaeologist so this is her forte and something she enjoys. However, Chris wanted to join in but was a bit gung-ho and was messing up the holes, which frustrated Deb as she had a plan and was on schedule and knew what she was doing. Oops.

Just before any group leaves Matang, they are asked to do a presentation in front of all the management team available on the day, plus Keith and Caroline. This gives the volunteers a chance to reflect on, and take pride in, what they have achieved during their time here, and if they have any recommendations which may enhance the future of the centre or the experience of future groups of volunteers. Also, it makes you realise what you have learned, and what you will be taking away with you, experience wise. Who knows, you may decide to volunteer at another project somewhere and share ideas with other volunteers, benefiting other animals and keepers.

With this in mind, I invited all the girls over for the evening, to get together and come up with a plan as to how we wanted to present our experience. Once we had come up with an idea of how our presentation would go, we finished by looking through a photo album of Keith's that he had leant us, showing some of the history of the centre and some fantastic photographs he had taken of the animals over that last 2 years. When Keith had left the photo album for me, he had also left a bottle of beer as a surprise treat. Deb also brought beer when they all came over so, added to the sneaky beer I had earlier from Keith, I felt a little bit tiddly by the end of the evening. It doesn't take much when you haven't had any for a while and the heat of the place combine. As a third treat this evening, Leanne had some MP3 speakers so we were able to share my music playlist from home. It went down very well and a couple of the girls asked if they could have copies of it later.

Towards the end of the night only myself, Leanne and Deb remained, chatting on the verandah, happy with music, beer and a good plan for our presentation. We suddenly became aware that some rather large bugs had joined us on the verandah and couldn't help but spend ages laying on the floor with our cameras, getting macro shots of them. Zooming into the photos afterwards was incredible, the detail was absolutely amazing and fascinating. One was a cricket, I believe, which had a head like a dinosaur, watching me, and above his legs were what looked like little small green peas, which in a cricket could be its ears! I have included a photo of this one. The other was a large green beetle with Gossamer translucent wings and big yellow-orange eyes. We had never seen such large and amazing insects.

Before we knew it, it was 1 o'clock in the morning. We had lots in common, chatted so easily, a great night. I shall really miss this group when they leave.

I was alone in the house tonight, Heather being out and about again, but I had no visit from Martin so all seems right with the Slow Loris house. I did however, notice the cat up on the sink twice. That solves the haunted sponge mystery then! The cat knocks it off the sink.

First thing each morning at work, we all gather on the terrace in front of the Centre to find out what our rota is for that day. Ting San also joins the meeting, having her morning exercise in a little play area designed for her, just in front of the terrace. She decided this morning to come over to me, took my hand and then promptly led me off to play with her. I was very honoured indeed to be her entertainment and playmate for a while.

The enrichment of the day was grass filled puzzle buckets for the macaques, which kept Matty busy again and worked well. Sandra wanted to help build Emily's 'nest box' today and had lots of advice to give on how it should be done, so I let her run with it as her project. It is great to see people who have no animal experience previously, come alive and buzz with ideas and passion, often thinking totally out of the box and coming up with ideas that are a real curve ball but are brilliant. As animal keepers, you are always trying to come up with fresh enrichment but sometimes do find yourselves getting stuck in a rut of thinking. Having people come along with novel ideas gives us a whole new perspective too, so even as an experienced animal keeper you will return home with new ideas and directions to go down. Everyone's a winner and the animals all do well out of it too. Having Sandra's help meant Emily had her box quicker for a start. With the wood being so hard to cut all help is very much appreciated to speed up the process.

Heather was back by the evening and kindly cooked for us both, then it was an early night ready for our first escapade out of the centre, bright and early in the morning. We were going Kayaking with the "Kuching Kayak Sdn Bhd" , and I couldn't wait. We had booked Mr Boon (Heather's usual taxi driver) to pick us up at 7am. Mr Boon was a lovely man, working long hours to support his family with an aim to fund his childrens' paths through university. Always happy and chatty being very good at English Mr Boon proved invaluable to all the volunteers. I still have his business card, having kept it just in case I got the opportunity to return some day.

Morning dawned and Mr Boon arrived promptly at 6.30am! I learned later that Mr Boon is ALWAYS early, which is far better than being late! It is Malaysian etiquette that you should always use a persons title such as Mr or Mrs when addressing them. The cabs bear the livery of Kuching City Taxis the cars being painted in a bright red along the sides and bumpers, with a bright yellow roof and bonnet. They can be found at a taxi rank outside one of the main hotels of Kuching. Mr Boon drove us into Kuching and once there we waited at Singgahsana for our 8.30am pickup, which turned up at 8.15am! I had been aware of the phrase "rubber time" in other countries but had always thought that this generally meant "laid back and late", rather than early – but not here!

It was an hours drive to the Borneo Highlands where we were going to be kayaking, stopping at Mama's Bakery on the way for some amazing little cakes and pastries to pack for lunch. The scenery through the highlands was stunning, with big cliff domes, like Spion Kops, dominating the skyline. We were to be making our way down the *sungai Semadang* (Semadang River) in 2 person kayaks. After donning our lifejackets and receiving a bit of instruction from the tour guide of how to stay safe and what we would be experiencing, Deb and I, being of a similar height and build decided to buddy up and took off in one kayak. Leanne and Chris climbed into the other one and set off behind us. My technique of rowing hadn't improved much since my last attempt in Australia a few years ago. I steered us into the trees twice and we got covered in foliage, but at least we didn't stop for a break on a 'Crocodile Nesting Area' or capsize in the river (with said Crocodiles) as I did in Australia! But that's another story altogether. A large bark cornet dropped into the boat on one of our forays towards the trees, where the bark had dried and curled off the tree like a giant pencil shaving falling from a pencil sharpener. I took it back with me as a souvenir of our trip and actually managed to bring it home, where I had it as a 'treasure' for many years. A couple of sections of the river saw us battling with rapids of differing degrees of intensity, but we all managed them admirably. Our guide, Jurry, was in a one man kayak and definitely 'eye candy' for the girls it turned out. He was a lovely looking guy, and really nice too. Everyone here is so friendly and laid back, its wonderful. We stopped after about 45 minutes and moored up by a small Bidayuh village for a tour around. The village was called Kampung Danu and stunning in its simple, proud, formal gardens and seating areas. It had a grand wooden clik-clak bridge as a mainland entrance which was built for the millenium. Prior to this bridge being constructed it was the traditional style, consisting of long lengths of bamboo strapped together in a particular method like a triangle or 'V'shape – very precarious to walk across, and I wouldn't have wanted to carry anything over it. Maybe you just ran for it and the momentum kept you from slipping off.

Many, many fruits and veg are grown here, such as pineapple, chillies, durian, cocoa, dragon fruit, lime, aubergine, marrow, coconut etc. Again, they used to have a longhouse but times have changed and the people now all have their own houses. Sadly, or not, this was a completely unspoilt village that Jurry knew of and so there were no souvenirs or anything to buy at all. It was in the middle of nowhere and that was nice but in later years the village has become connected to Kuching via a main road and visitors can now experience homestays here, living alongside the small community of families and helping with the harvesting of their crops.

Returning to our Kayaks after the village tour we travelled down the river some more before settling on a small beach for lunch and a swim. The limestone cliffs over the other side of the river were awesome, with grey birds flying low across the water. Jurry pointed out a large bees nest high in a tree and also told us there are apparently 60 different species of bamboo in this area. Included in the tour were photos of us on our expedition, taken by Jurry, which we could download online once we returned.

One final stretch after lunch and it was over too quickly, although Jurry told us we had rowed 26km in around 3 hours! I can't see that being the case but then I am rubbish at distances, especially kilometres. The peace and quiet and beauty of the area were hard to leave behind. Back on dry land we were shown a portable shower on the pavement, where we could get washed and changed before heading back to Kuching.

On our return we all decided to hit the shops and it was almost good timing on the way back, but not quite. The heavens opened, and continued to rain heavily from then on in. We got absolutely soaked, Deb and I killing ourselves laughing as we fought bravely through the monsoon, back to Singgahsana. Mr Boon picked us up at 8pm but the roads were completely flooded and impassable meaning we couldn't get past Matang Jaya and were forced to turn back to Kuching to stay overnight. Still absolutely soaked from earlier we were feeling pretty cold but had no dry clothes on us at all. I didn't fancy staying in a dormitory room as we had no pyjamas, no toothbrush, no dry clothes or warm tops, so Deb and I decided to splash out (about £30) and go get ourselves a cosy room at the Hilton Hotel. We each bought a bright orange Singgahsana polo shirt to change into before bravely trudging back out into the storm to walk the 10 minutes over to the Hilton. We must have looked ridiculous when we arrived at reception but we booked ourselves in, shopped for some toothbrushes and milk for a cup of tea, then retired to our room for a wonderfully hot shower before heading to the bar wearing our still wet work trousers, matching orange backpacker polo shirts and no underwear. Talk about stand out and feel rather underdressed. Mind you, I still have that top and its almost as good as new 12 years on, so it was fantastic quality it turns out. Karaoke was in full swing in the bar as we settled on a couple of stools at a table near the window and enjoyed the entertainment, together with a few drinks before returning to our room. It was 1.30am by this time and we needed to be up and away at 5.30am to rejoin the others ready for Mr Boon to take us back to MWC. The beds were comfortable and we slept well.

We were a bit rushed checking out of the hotel and I unintentionally left my carton of milk on the Hilton Reception Desk, knowing Mr Boon is bound to be early!

I later discovered that this overnight last minute decision impulse of grandeur could have cost me my relationship back at home as, unbeknownst to me, the Hilton then sent a bill to my home address for items used in the mini bar in our room. We hadn't had anything out of the mini bar, knowing how much they cost worldwide. It did look very suspect though, a hotel for the night, with another woman, and apparent emptying of the mini bar in the room. Luckily, I have an understanding and trusting partner who, after a little frostiness, did believe me that it was a twin room and we were purely friends caught in a storm. Phew!

The roads had cleared luckily and so we were able to return to Matang, arriving at our biliks for 7.45am, so enough time for a quick cuppa and change of clothes before heading off to work. It continued to rain throughout the day so I decided against joining the overnight forest trek Tim had organised for us. I was very tired and really didn't fancy getting wet through a second night, and sleeping rough with my contact lenses in again would not be a good idea. The other 3 who had booked to go previously (Leanne, Deb and Gill) still went, which meant they needed to leave work early to prepare for the night. The rest of us carried on with the tasks of the day before Heather took us shopping in the evening and we all had the usual Roti Ciani and Mango Lasse. A feast of a meal that cost RM5, which was equal to 75p. I splashed out £1 on a bamboo mat for my bedroom and yesterday bought some MP3 speakers so I am really making myself at home and nest building! This place is getting to me and I feel very settled. I just hope the next group are as easy to get on with. As I settled down into my newly mat bedecked bedroom I hoped the others would manage to stay dry in the forest camp. At least its warm tonight.

I received reports from back home that my mum isn't happy with my having a traditional tattoo. I think she imagined it being done by a loin-clothed native in a mud hut, with sharp bamboo tips, dipped in berry juice and that gangrene will set in! I do have a bit of a reputation where I promise my mum I won't do anything wreckless or stupid and then very often do do something wreckless or stupid, including the worlds highest bungee jump. Hopefully I can reassure her that I am perfectly safe and there was no risk involved in the tattoo. Twelve years on and the images of my tattoos are still as sharp as the day they were done, showing how much of an artist Ernesto was.

"One's destination is never a place, but always a new way of seeing things"

Henry Miller

CHAPTER SEVEN

"We wander for distraction, but we travel for fulfillment"

Hillary Belloc

It's the 25th day of my adventures in Borneo and, after working the morning, we're all off to visit Bako National Park for the weekend - a place that would become one of my favourite places in the world. Tim kindly drove us to *Kampung Bako* (Bako village) to pick up the boat. The boat journey itself was fun, if a little hair-raising. It took about 30 minutes, bouncing at high speed out into the South China Sea with lifejackets neatly folded, and sealed, in a big bag at the front. As we approached Bako National Park, the boat shut off its engine and we were told to grab all our possessions, and wade in to shore. We initially thought they were having a joke with us but then realised that the tide was out and it was too shallow to actually get any closer to land. It was quite a distance we had to wade but the scenery was absolutely stunning already so we kept our bags and cameras high above our heads, like commandos on an assault mission, and set off. It all helped add to the experience of remoteness. As we walked out of the sea onto the beach at *Teluk Asam* (Asam Bay), feeling like we were now castaways, we spotted the Park Headquarters and headed off to book in. There were all 6 of us volunteers plus Caroline, sharing a chalet. We were booked into Chalet No.5, the last one along the park on the right, before it wound around the corner. Somehow Caroline's booking hadn't registered though, maybe because she was not staying the full weekend as we were, so we only had a 6 bed chalet. Caroline was fine with it and happy to spend the night on the floor in our room, only staying the one night anyway. Everyone donated their blankets and I had taken my bamboo mat so she ended up like the princess and the pea with all the layers to sleep on and probably comfier than any of us.

The chalet was raised up on stilts above the ground with steps leading up to a large verandah at the front with plenty of wooden chairs to sit out on and a wooden table if you wanted to eat outside. The chalet itself had 2 bedrooms, each with 3 beds in, and a huge bathroom which had a separate (cold) shower and a western style toilet. The waste bin was unusual as it was a metal pedal bin that had been firmly attached to the floor. When you pressed the pedal and peered inside there wasn't actually a bottom to the bin, or a floor to the chalet. Whatever you threw in there fell down directly into a black rubber dustbin way below the house! Ingenious. The bathroom also had a small fridge in, which was handy, if a little bizarre. Once settled in we went for a walk along the Teluk Paku trail (Paku is an edible fern and very delicious), which takes about an hour and passes through the cliff forests, along sturdy boardwalks winding through the mangroves and ending at a beautiful secluded little beach. This is one of the best routes for spotting Proboscis Monkeys. We heard some grunting in the treetops but it was the wrong time of day to see them properly.

Proboscis monkeys are one of my favourites that are only found in Borneo and in danger of becoming extinct due to palm oil plantations destroying their habitat. They are a large primate, with the male weighing up to around 23kg and about 30" tall. They have partially webbed feet making them excellent swimmers both above and below the water. Proboscis monkeys are famous for their very large pendulous noses in the males – females have smaller, upturned noses. The body and face are a deep red colour with a mop of darker hair on their heads. They have grey arms and legs with white hands and feet. The tail is also a white colour with a black tip. Eating mainly young leaves, buds and shoots they have a large pot belly and, like cows and Colobus monkeys, they ruminate to aid digestion (regurgitate food to digest a second time). This practice leads to a lot of wind!

We did see the first of many Bornean Bearded Pigs, snuffling around the place, as well as lots of long-tailed macaques, mudskippers and the large pincher arms of sky-blue fiddler crabs wiggling above the sand, like white 'V's or flags of surrender.

At Park Headquarters there is also a canteen selling simple but good food 3 times a day, a picnic area, shower and toilets, and a little shop where you can purchase items such as tinned food, rice, sugar and other essentials. We all stopped at the canteen and had a plateful of rice, curry and vegetables plus a good cup of *kopi* (coffee), then booked a night walk with some local guides for that evening. During our guided walk there were lots of little things to see, such as spiders, frogs, luminous fungi, geckos, hermit crabs, catfish, stick insects (huge ones) and a finale of a tree full of fireflys but sadly we didn't see any large stuff that were possible here, like Slow Loris, Timpard cat, Civet or Pangolin unfortunately. To add to this disappointment, I had forgotten to put any insect repellant on AND had also committed the most important gaff of going out in a t-shirt rather than long sleeves. Serves me right, I was absolutely bitten to hell and was covered in huge red lumps all over my arms and neck. Very attractive, as you can see in the photo section!

One thing I did think was lovely was that local beliefs say Fireflies are the souls of their ancestors, having their last cigarette before moving on, and its the butt of the cigarette that is glowing, not the butt of the fly!

The next morning we arose at 5.45 so we were ready and in place to see the Proboscis Monkeys emerge from the forest around 6.30am. Caroline, Deb and myself moved further up the trail, having sussed it out the day before, away from everyone else, as many other visitors had joined us with the same idea. We were the first to hear them approach and catch a glimpse of them in their palm tree aerial walkways. I think we all held our breath, not wanting to disturb them and enjoy this privilege, before re-joining the others on the boardwalk and continuing to watch the monkeys tuck into their breakfast in the mangroves.

Back to the canteen for breakfast, which this time consisted of rice, noodles, sausage, egg, fishcake. The chips had all gone but I think rice and noodles are carbs enough for one meal really. The meal was finished off with the usual bright green cake! A favourite colour for food here is green, whether it be bread, cake, jam, dumplings, sweets – all bright green. Apparently the green colour comes from the fragrant juice extracted from the Pandan (screw-pine) plants. An essential ingredient in Asian cuisine which is equivalent to our popular use of vanilla essence in our cuisine.

Still on a high from our early morning encounters on Teluk Paku and fully revitalised from our hearty breakfast, Leanne, Caroline and I wanted to explore Bako further and decided to do the loop trail around the park. There are several trails to follow and this one we understood to include every kind of terrain and vegetation in Bako and only taking around 45 minutes to walk. This was ideal as Caroline was heading back lunchtime with Sandra and Chris, so needed to catch the boat. The actual walk we found ourselves on however, turned out to be 5½km long and, when we checked the board later was meant to take 4-5 hours. We managed to do it in 3½ hours. This was the Lintang and Bukit Tambi Trail, taking in most of the differing landscapes of Bako by climbing up steep rickety steps or following hill paths with natural steps of tangled roots from the Kerangas (Heath Forest). The views at the top of the island, looking across to Mount Santabong and the little deserted sandy bays below were truly spectacular and well worth the arduous climb. I was totally amazed how my body achieved it, considering my normal capabilities, especially in humid heat. We came across many different kinds of pitcher plants, a blue spiders web and a couple of waterfalls. The top of the park was a weird mix of smooth rock, scrub and shrubs, black boulders and moonscapes. Thinking it was only a 45 minute trail I had again been silly, and not taken any kind of drink with me. Luckily, Caroline had an isotonic drink which she very kindly eeked out and shared with me. We pushed ourselves to catch the boat for Caroline and did get back a little late but luckily they had waited and the other girls had brought Caroline's bags from the chalet so she was all ready to hop aboard straight away. The tide was in so the boat could reach the jetty this time too so there was no wading out involved.

Relaxing after a nice refreshing shower when we returned to the chalet I remember thinking how the shower was so much better than my usual 'jug and mandi' routine for sure! We wanted to catch some sightings of Proboscis again as they head back to the forest at dusk but sadly we had missed them, they had gone early at around 4 o'clock. Fancied an early night it seems, or maybe had just had a particularly large feed that day and needed to sit back and digest it all in their big pot-belly stove like tummies. Instead of the Proboscis monkeys we watched the long-tailed macaques playing before bedtime, I do so love macaques and their close social system. I could watch them for hours. What I didn't enjoy watching was people feeding them chocolate pillows. It appears its the same the world over, people feeling the need to interfere with wildlife rather than enjoy its uniqueness. I thought back to the 'tip' of miming a catapult to scare them away from this unsuitable food option but couldn't bring myself to do it.

At the end of the boardwalk there was a wooden shelter, like a bus stop, which had steps down into the mangroves. We decided to investigate, finding some secluded little caves amongst giant sandstone boulders as well as spotting lots of mudskippers, blue crabs, red crabs and crabs snapping in shallow rock pools. We also came across a tubby English couple, boring their Malay guide by explaining different types of mortgages – poor chap! We spent a while taking photographs while we waited for the area around the Park Headquarters to be 'fogged' to clear insects. This is a regular procedure they have to do as the mosquito population is massive (see picture of my arm earlier!). I believe this is to combat the Aedis mosquito, which is known to transmit Dengue fever, and still common in areas of Malaysia. The larvae develop around sources of standing water such as drains, pots, ponds etc. A couple of pest controllers get suited up and cover the area with a thick fog of insecticide, so we are all banished from the area until the fog drifts away over the sea. Once it was cleared though it was time for food again, it was 6.30pm and we had worked up an appetite. Once fed we returned to our chalet and relaxed on the verandah with some beer and my music, chatting about the many sights and experiences of the day. The evening ended with an enormous show of sheet lightening and the sound of rolling thunder. Their was no rain to accompany this wonderful spectacle of nature which surprised me. I always expect rain when there is thunder and lightening, particularly in a rainforest. But no, not a drop to be had!

The following morning, and the last day of our trip, turned out to be the best day by far. We were up early again to see if we could catch the Proboscis monkeys but they decided to allude us again and decided not to come down to the water today. Instead, we walked on a bit and saw some up in the trees in the distance, but not for long. Disappointed, we toddled back for our camp breakfast of the usual mix of rice, chips, sausage, egg, fishcake and, of course, the slice of bright green cake! Meals are good here despite warnings to the contrary and their obvious randomness. Full bellies and it was back to the chalet for showers and to pack, ready for our 11am checkout time.

Deb and I decided we would then have time to finish off the trip with one more walk, a visit to Paku Beach as Deb said she had read up on it and it was well worth seeing. By this time I was so at home in Bako and Borneo itself, I was going native, scrabbling around the trails quite comfortably in my sandals and flip flops – who needs heavy walking boots and socks!? Arriving at the beach we were not disappointed, it was awesome, with a little bit of everything. The sand was white and strewn with pieces of drift wood, fallen old tree trunks with fungus on, chiselled boulders like the moon, crashing waves, more shells than you could shake a stick at, commanding cliff faces topped with trees and palms and, the icing on the cake, Proboscis monkeys playing in the trees. We couldn't believe it. Unfortunately, we didn't have long as it was approaching checkout time and our boat was booked for 12 noon. We wished we had found this hidden treasure earlier on our trip. But, we had seen it and we were extremely happy with that. As we returned along the track, magic of all magic, we happened to spot a flying lemur clinging to a tree. It looked yellowy brown in colour with spatulate back legs. I never imagined I'd see one of them, especially during the daytime. It looked healthy and I tried to get a photo of it, but sadly the photo came out very blurred when I checked it later. A bit further along the path we then saw a group of Proboscis playing in the trees again. Then, when on the boardwalk, we literally bumped into 3 male proboscis either side of the balustrade and so close I could have shook hands with them and tickled their tubby tummies! I could have cried – what a finale! The males were grunting and waggling their pendulous noses but were far too busy eating to bother about one another too much. LOTS of pictures and video snippets later and time was getting on. We were both in total awe and blown away by this encounter but Deb very kindly let me stay watching them whilst she went back to get our bags and tell the others of the sighting. Really nice of her. One by one though they had their fill and the proboscis tiptoed across the water to dry land and away into the bushes. The others were gutted, having missed it all by 5-10 minutes.

Jenny then spotted a troop of Silver Leafed Monkeys (also known as Silvery Langurs), including a mum and bright orange baby. The babies are born bright orange to stand out as being vulnerable, so the whole troop can be aware of them and protect them in any dangerous situations. As they mature the colouration changes to that of the adults, which is a kind of salt and pepper style of grey/silver and black. They are long, lanky primates, similar to gibbons and spider monkeys. I thought we had missed seeing them, having previously heard they were in the area. So crazy how everything came at the last minute, making it so hard to leave. What an amazing place, definitely somewhere I would love to return to one day.

The boatman had already arrived to collect us, arriving around 2 hours early actually. I thought Mr Boon was early with his timings, but 2 hours! Maybe it was because of the tide times to come into shore. Anyway, he was all ready and waiting to take us back to Kampung Bako. This boat had a red and white striped canopy to protect us from the Sun – very posh, and seemed a much more sedate affair than our arrival! Landing at Bako village we relaxed with a coffee and waited for the next bone-shaker bus back to Kuching. It only cost RM2 each and took about an hour, dropping us outside the Post Office. We headed back to Singgahsana to catch up on emails, drop off our baggage and get a drink. We also snuck in a crafty shower and change of clothes before then meeting up with Heather at the Coffee Bean Cafe for a coffee and a cake. Returning to Singgahsana once more, we dozed on the cushioned, bamboo platform in reception area for an hour, to wait for Tim to drive us back to Matang. Stopping off at the Banana Leaf for dinner we then returned home to 'the street'. We had been invited to an evening of playing monopoly at Jambu Restaurant, but really didn't fancy that as an evenings entertainment after the wonders of Bako National Park. How could anything top that, and we were very tired anyway.

It's been 27 days and I realise I have now travelled on all means of transport since beginning my trip – plane, train, car, people carrier, taxi, bus, kayak and speedboat – impressive. Maybe I should seek out a hot air balloon trip while I'm here.

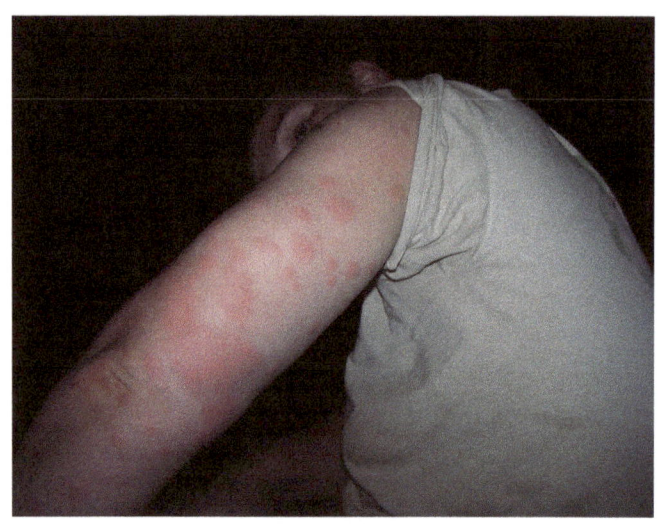

My arm covered in insect bites!

Proboscis Monkey
Bako National Park

Bako Village

Beautiful Bako National Park

"The real voyage of discovery consists not in seeing new landscapes, but in having new eyes"

Marcel Proust

CHAPTER EIGHT

"A good traveller has no fixed plan and is not intent on arriving"

Lao Tzu

More trips out were planned the following day with Tim. We are having a real adventure holiday week this week.

The morning was spent visiting Semenggoh Rehabilitation Centre, within the Wildlife Centre of the Semenggoh Nature Reserve. The centre was set up in 1975 in order to help wild animals, found as illegal pets or injured within the forests, with a goal to rehabilitate and hopefully release them back into the wild, whilst also researching via captive breeding programmes for endangered species and educating visitors regarding the importance of conservation within Sarawak and beyond. The Centre has been a huge success with many species of endangered mammals, birds and reptiles but it is the orangutans who attract the most interest. The programme has been so successful that the centre and its surrounding reserves have reached their capacity for releasing orangutans so Semenggoh works hand in hand with

Matang Wildlife Centre (part of Kubah National Park) for continued rehabilitation work. I was told during my stay that 23 orangutans had been successfully released into this semi-wild lifestyle but this number could be hugely different now. This is how Aman became a resident at Matang. He was at Semenggoh, as previously covered, but had to be moved as he was an adult male (known as a 'cheekpadder' due to the large cheek pads male orangs develop as they reach maturity) and therefore clashed with another adult male residing there called Richie. Males are solitary and do not normally come into contact with other adult males but Richie had in fact bitten off one of Amans fingers in a scuffle. It is believed also that Aman's cataracts came about due to him biting through an electricity cable by accident. Of course, with poor eyesight and a male foe in his vicinity it would have been unsafe for Aman to remain in a semi-free forested environment so Matang was the only option for him. This also, of course, then gave him the opportunity for the cataract surgery to restore his eyesight. Still, knowing where he came from I can really feel his frustration being stuck in an enclosure where the viewing platform for visitors is above the top of his wall. No animal likes to be looked down on and laughed at by visitors. However, his enclosure was being kitted out with amazing multi level platforms and ropes to give him a birds-eye view and make him as happy and stimulated as possible. At least he could climb up and be eye level with visitors, although that then brought the added frustration of being able to see across into the unattainable forest beyond.

At Semenggoh we gathered on a large sloping wooden viewing platform which was similar in style to the stands at a football stadium, and watched as Joseph climbed onto a raised platform in the forest directly ahead of us and called the orangutans in for a scheduled supplemental feed. We were lucky to see two mums and babies, one adolescent female (older daughter) and a male. In time, orangs become totally self proficient in the forest and no longer need this feed, so it becomes an important gauge of how well the individuals are doing. Joseph is due to come to Matang to work with Ting San and the others on their rehabilitation path. He is very experienced in orangutan care and will be a huge asset to the team. It was lovely to watch him and how easy and natural he was as they all gathered around him for the feed. It was amazing to see just how many bananas each orang could carry away with them too. I saw one with 5 bananas in her mouth, sticking out like big fat yellow cigars, plus 2 or 3 grasped tightly in hands and feet as she made her way into the canopy to eat them in peace. The whole forest area was strung with miles of thick ropes, to represent liana vines, for the orangs to be able to traverse the treetops with ease and safety as they learned to adapt back into a wild, natural way of life. Orangutans are much endangered nowadays as they can only be found in Borneo and Sumatra (2 differing species). With the modern world seeking cheap food and resources, the rainforests where they live are fast becoming extinct, being replaced by Palm Oil plantations which are no use to any of the native wildlife. Animals such as orangutans are slaughtered, with the babies being sold as pets or kept as pets locally in dire conditions. Several excellent charitable organisations are desperately trying to turn this trend around but with the rainforest disappearing at a huge pace each day, there is becoming nowhere to return any rescued animals to. In 2017 it was estimated that the rainforest was being cut down at a rate of a football pitch every second of every day, 365 days per year. An unimaginable and shocking figure. Lets hope that people will soon realise that palm oil is in fact causing us harm too and a new, more sustainable and ethical alternative can be found, before its too late. Sorry, small rant over. Back to the adventure.

On the way back from Semmenggoh we stopped at Mama's Bakery to get some of their delicious warm savoury buns (like when we went kayaking) – love them sooo much. Then it was back to Kuching for lunch before heading to our afternoon destination - the Fairy Caves, known locally as Gua Pari. These are within the Bau region, about 50km from Kuching with a beautiful drive along roads passing through rubber estates, pepper gardens and cocoa plantations. The Fairy Caves are free as, due to dangers involved in scrabbling around the caves themselves, Sarawak Forestry will not take responsibility for any accidents that may occur. To access the caves there is a concrete tower, which houses 4 double flights of concrete steps. It looked like a mine shaft or external steps to a multi storey car park attached to the outside of the caves. Once you reached the entrance you were then faced with more steps, although these were rickety wooden ones, making you then start to feel the fairyland enchantment. The cave roof here was quite low too so the approach was quite eerie and dark, although not too dark that you needed a torch.

As we arrived at the top of these steps we at last emerged into a huge cavern of twisting pathways and concrete steps with moss, ferns and other greenery making the scene inside spectacular. The foliage thrived due to constant dripping water from the cave mouth, 30m above the ground, and the guano of the bats living within the cave. Viewing platforms had been built to allow you the chance to capture this place on camera but you really couldn't do it justice or explain how beautiful, and huge, it was. It was like a scene inside one of those Chinese bottle ornaments. It WAS like fairy land! A huge cave mouth opened up into the sky and you could hear the bats in the cave that would, at nightfall, come streaming out. Some of the rock formations around the cave apparently looked like certain Buddhist and Taoist deities and you would see Incense Sticks pushed into crevices around these formations, as offerings of worship. I have read that, during Japanese occupation of the state in 1941, the caves were used by the Japanese army to defend themselves so some parts of the cave are actually remnants of fortresses built by them.

We spent all afternoon walking around, exploring the Fairy Caves, and Tim also dared us to climb through small tunnels and holes to a tiny, little round cavern, just big enough to sit in. Most of us took up the challenge and felt great for doing it. I was the first one through the rocks to crouch inside this tiny Chamber so was able to enjoy the full effect. With a central rock formation support giving it the appearance of being inside a snail shell, it was very special and so didn't feel claustrophobic at all. We then carried on exploring some of the bigger caverns and climbed out onto a beautifully carved, Asian style wooden viewing platform at the cave mouth to enjoy views over the fields below, before having to return to the bus. We were **absolutely filthy** but all thoroughly enjoyed it.

Once we arrived back at Matang it was time for Jenny to sadly say goodbye. She was carrying on her adventure by flying to the Philippines to teach English to local children there. I went over to the girls' bilik for a drink and to relive the wonderful day we had just had. Time flew and it was 1.30am before we knew it. This seems to be a regular timeframe we seem to be habituated to!

It was the final morning of work. We carried out our usual duties of Quarantine, Ting Sans bedroom and the deer, then did our group presentation to Tim and Caroline. Sadly no-one from SFC could make it but at least we didn't have a large official audience to worry about. Sandra and Jenny had put together a really good presentation on Aqil's laptop and Chris stepped up to talk it through. It all went well, group photos were taken and then it was all back to bilik street to freshen up, change our clothes and pack, before driving into Kuching ready for Deb and I to get tattoos done at Headhunters. I texted my niece, Laura, for her 18th birthday while I was there, as I couldn't get through by phone. My tattoo was a little more painful, being on my ankle, but still totally comfortable and enjoyable. The finished piece looks amazing and has such power for me. I mustn't have any more!! Ernesto told me where to buy my own set of tattoo instruments, avoiding tourist tacky ones. He drew them on a piece of paper for me, so I knew exactly what to look for. I wasn't intending to use them you understand, but I felt it would be a really fitting souvenir that represented an important part of my trip, and my life here, to take home and keep me attached to Borneo in some way. I did find a lovely set and bartered the price down a bit to RM160. The shop owner tried to sell me a box set tourist 'tat' version but I wanted a real set as this was such a special thing for me.

For our last night we all met up for a meal at Top Spot Food Court – a restaurant of several businesses vying for custom, situated on the top of a multi-storey car park. Luckily the lifts were working to take us to the top, as this can sometimes be an issue, or of course you can hike up the 6 storeys of steps and work up a good appetite. As you arrive at the top you are met by stall upon stall around the outer edges of the car park, with brightly lit neon signs advertising who each vendor is, and a stall number. There are no menus you just walk along, studying the vast array of fresh fish and accompanying vegetables before deciding which stall seems to offer the best food to suit your taste. We wouldn't have had a clue what to do if we didn't have Tim with us to guide us through the process. He helped us to order an array of dishes which we shared between us, so we could experience as many flavours as possible. Once you have placed your order you try to sit at a table as near to the chosen stall/s as possible and wait for them to bring over your food once it is prepared. This wasn't always possible so how they found everyone in the mass of tables and people I don't know. The order did come in dribs and drabs but we didn't mind that as there was no rush, we knew it was fresh and it made for a very relaxed atmosphere where we could chat away happily, with conversations diverted to each new dish that was presented to us as they arrived. Being on top of a multi-storey car park, you can imagine how large this area was. Sadly I didn't take any photographs of Top Spot but you will find them on Facebook and TripAdvisor with many pictures of the experience from other visitors. Well worth looking at.

We were all staying at Singgahsana overnight so finished off our evening upstairs in the bar, playing pool and choosing the music (Blur, Doors, Faithless). It was a sad end to a truly amazing experience, where strangers had come together from all walks of life, worked and lived together in a totally alien environment, and made a little bit of difference to some endangered animals. We drank a little bit too much and stayed up a little bit too late but it was really good fun as our last night. We of course wrote on the wall of the bar, as is tradition.

Putting in a load of laundry to be done while I was here, I eventually got to bed at 2.30am.

I was sharing a room with Deb so I made sure I was awake again at 5.30am to see her off. She really didn't want to go bless her – having got the bug for Borneo like I have. Maybe we would all return one day and see how the centre has progressed under the guidance of WOX and The Great Orangutan Project. I hope so.

Gill was next to leave at around 7am, travelling on to Thailand and then Leanne was off at teatime, for her flight home back to the UK. Very sad to see them all go.

"When we get out of the glass bottle of our ego and when we escape like the squirrels in the cage of our personality and get into the forest again, we shall shiver with cold and fright. But things will happen to us so that we don't know ourselves. Cool, unlying life will rush in"

D H Simon

CHAPTER NINE

"Travel is glamorous only in retrospect"
Paul Thereaux

Meeting Heather for breakfast before collecting my laundry (how quick is that service?!), we headed back to Matang as both of us were due to work this afternoon. As it turned out, the afternoon proved to be rather eventful.

Heather started the ball rolling by accidentally taking a strong sleeping tablet instead of a normal malaria tablet. She was like a drunk person, mumbling and trying desperately to fight it, staggering around and almost falling into her laundry bucket! The trouper that she is though managed to stay awake and make it to work knowing it was only the two of us on shift, taking over from Keith and Caroline.

As we arrived, Caroline emerged from the animal area a bit shaken. She was just coming out from the forest, only to come across Kevin the pig-tailed macaque, who had escaped from his enclosure yet again. Apparently he had bitten her trousers whilst she had Ting San with her. The only thing to do was throw a pot of seeds in his direction to keep him busy foraging and then leg it back to the centre. All was OK and no-one was hurt so normal service was resumed and Caroline then left to have the afternoon off and relax.

Before I made a start on my chores I thought it wise to follow Heather back up into the forest with Ting San, to make sure she was OK and would arrive safely in the platform and exercise area, purpose built for training Orangutans to survive in the wild. There was Kevin, sitting on the boardwalk outside his gate. I walked towards him and he took hold of my hands, stood on his back legs and nibbled at me very gently, which is a macaque greeting, then sat peacefully at my feet. I couldn't see where he had got out but luckily he followed me down the path and back towards the centre so I could locate James and get him to come and unlock the enclosure to let Kevin back in. This worked a treat, thank goodness, as representatives from CITES (Convention on International Trade in Endangered Species of Wild Fauna and Flora) came on a visit of the Centre with Tim ten minutes later! We just hoped that Kevin and his fellow macaques wouldn't decide to find the escape route again in the meantime.

It seemed all of the animals were in a funny mood – they seemed very tense about something that was unbeknown to me. Maybe they were confused because there were no other volunteers around and we haven't in fact been around much at all this week, due to visiting local attractions. Not only was Kevin being out on the loose again, but Tim the deer's glands on his face were inflamed and he was stamping his feet as he walked, Boboy was wanting to bite me manicly and Matty was definitely giving me the cold shoulder. However, they all settled down and returned to normal half an hour later, once I had settled back into my routine and they knew I was going to be sticking around. All was forgiven! Maybe it was the CITES official visitors or maybe the storm that is brewing. We shall never know. Animals are so attuned to their environment and the subtle changes that may occur and knock it off balance for a while.

Heather made it through the afternoon bless her, I don't know how. That is true grit and determination but I bet the afternoon seemed never ending for her
.
Tim praised my work with the animals saying they are much calmer since I've been there and I have a great way with them. He also thinks I'm good with people, which is something I have never been confident about so that was really lovely to hear. Great praise indeed so I was well chuffed and so nice of him to take the time to tell me this. I am certainly enjoying working in-situ and with Heather and other volunteers also making me feel valued, I may have found my niche and a new path to follow!

Once work was finished Heather made a start on her packing, as she too was leaving tomorrow, and cooked us our final meal together of chicken curry. I will really miss her when she has gone as I have learned so much from her and enjoyed her company immensely. I will have to look after myself from here on in and get to grips with cooking as decent meals as I can muster on the little 2 ring gas hob.

The general rule of volunteering is that, as people leave, you are free to raid their rooms for anything they may have left behind, be it clothing, food or such like. However, we did indeed have a huge rain storm so this put a stop to me checking out the now empty biliks on the street. I was happy with that though as the local residents then work hard to prepare the houses for the next set of volunteers, so it is only right that they should have the luxury of seeking out any left behind treasures worth commandeering.

The next day Heather and I are working all day again, so Heather invited me to join her and Ting San on the famous Pitcher Plant trail through the forest. I was delighted. However I couldn't wear my own walking boots, as they would cover my recent ankle tattoo and it needed to be uncovered for the first few days to heal properly. Deb had left behind some shoes which may fit me so I went to try them on. Big surprise though, there was a HUGE ants nest inside them so that was a definite no-no. Fortunately, sitting next to them and ant nest free, there was another pair, belonging to who knows, nearby. They were way too big for me but I tightened them up with the laces as best I could and they were comfortable enough. By the end of the day the toe section had curled up where my feet didn't reach and the shoes had bent over when I walked. I looked like Coco the clown!

Hurrying through my morning routine I then joined Heather and Ting San at the forest platform. What an amazing morning. We shared pieces of orange between the three of us before Ting San then started to gather branches and build a nest in front of us. Bored with that she then promptly decided to steal my bottle of water and drink it herself. She is such a comical character, and very smart. Heading off on the Pitcher Trail, Ting San was so sweet, holding my hand and walking with me most of the time as if she was taking care of me, knowing it was my first time and she knew the way. If she went ahead she either waited or came back for me, holding out her hand again. She would climb trees occasionally and seek out Kandis berries, also finding ginger, termite mounds and pitcher plants. You could see where the trail had been "Ting San'd" as many a tree or palm was either snapped or lay broken and bent across the path. She had learnt to bend trees, to travel from one to the next without needing to come down to the ground, which is a normal mode of locomotion for orangutans in the wild, but a fair few were rotten and she'd come crashing down. Luckily she was only climbing small shrubs and trees so didn't hurt herself at all, just rolled over, stunt-man style, and merrily climbed up the next one. She let me carry her when she was tired.

The path followed forests of Kerangas and Licuala palms with the ground shooting up abundant areas of pitcher plants. These are shaped liked pitcher jugs so I suppose that must where the jugs get their name. These particular ones are *Nepenthus ampullaria* and, as all pitcher plants do, they actually eat insects by trapping them inside the 'jug' and slowly digesting them. The soil around them is quite poor so this clever trick provides the plants with additional nutrients it needs in order to thrive.

Criss-crossing little creeks over small wooden plank bridges, we continued the trail through the forest of stilt-rooted trees, fan palms and pandanus plants, stepping over fallen tree trunks whilst all the time not believing how incredibly lucky I am to have such an intimate one to one experience with a baby orang in her natural habitat. I couldn't have had this anywhere else in the world and not even here at any other time. Normally the local keepers would take charge of orangutan rehabilitation and care but at this moment in time staff were short, we were in between carers for Ting San and I was a long term volunteer with a primate (and other wildlife) background knowledge and experience. The biggest privilege I will ever have for sure. We did have a small price to pay of course. I got 'leeched' a couple of times. I can only describe leeches as something like sticky bogeys when you're a kid, trying to flick them off your finger but finding they stick to each finger in turn and just won't go!! I was the lucky one though as Heather had 3 on her ankles when we got back – they wouldn't stop bleeding for ages as something in their saliva thins the blood for ease of extraction I believe.

In the afternoon, with my head still in the clouds, I got on with the behavioural enrichment for all the rescue centre animals before calling it a day and rushing back home to clean up and pack. I was going into Kuching with Heather, who is flying out tomorrow. I decided I might as well stay the Friday as well as I was due back there Saturday anyway to meet the new group of volunteers with Tim and the room costs the same as a Taxi to and from Matang. That means I'm here at Singgahsana once more, our home from home in Borneo, for 3 nights.

We met up with Sandra, Chris and Caroline and decided on a farewell meal at the Banana Leaf, but sadly it was closed for Dewali, so we went to Lyn's Thandoori instead, which was also scrummy as I recall, although I do still have a soft spot for eating my dinner off a banana leaf. We said our farewells to Sandra and Chris, wishing them all the best as they set off to the Canary Islands before joining a sailing crew on an Atlantic Crossing to the Dominican Republic. Wow, that's some adventure to take your mind off leaving the place we have all grown to love.

Caroline, Heather and I had one drink up in the roof space back in Singgahsana Lodge, overlooking Kuching's night sky, chatting about all we had accomplished this month and wondering if the next group will be as fun and enthusiastic. We really hope so. Checking our emails before bed we had all received an email from Deb, saying she had arrived home in the UK safely but had lost the memory card from her camera, with all her photos on. She was absolutely gutted and asked if we could all send what photos we had to her to try to compensate a bit. I can't imagine how she feels as she was so good at photography, having taken a few on my camera for me I could see she really had a good eye so her photos would have been amazing. I felt so sorry for her.

After breakfast the following morning I decided to hit the shops to do some serious gift shopping. However, nothing was open. Apparently they don't open until around 10am, but then they are open late into the evening so this makes perfect sense. I took a walk along the main *Jalan* (Road) but didn't really see anything of interest so returned to the Coffee Bean, a main coffee shop chain, and waited until the shops opened. I was then able to get some of my photos printed, top up my phone cards, buy a few presents and find a new backpack, as mine had a dodgy zip. I also bought new toe rings today and a new ankle bracelet, although I then managed to mend my old one and prefer that one! Once my shopping foray was complete I found a really pretty little Deli round the corner from Singgahsana where I tucked into a tuna sandwich. This was a toasted 3-tier affair with a little paper Malaysian flag on a cocktail stick placed through the middle to keep it in place. My latte coffee had two chocolate dust feathers on top. Both coffee and sandwich were extremely delicious.

Heading back to the hostel I set to catching up on emailing home and met the new group of volunteers as they arrived throughout the afternoon. We had two couples travelling together this time – Aaron & Cora, who were friends, and Gary & Karen, a married couple. The other two were girls travelling alone and called Sally and Penny. All the volunteers were from the UK and all seemed quite nice, although Penny (the youngest) may get a little annoying. My first impression was that I would probably like Aaron and Cora best as they were so easy to chat to, fun and chomping at the bit to get started, as I was.

Tim took us to Khatulistiwa for dinner then back to Singgahsana for the customary couple of drinks in the bar. All the staff at Singgahsana are using my name now, especially Richard – which is really nice and makes me feel even more as if I belong. I rang my Mum & Dad for a chat then called my sister, Steph, for a catchup before calling it a night. Steph very excitedly informed me that the date of her wedding had been set for 5th July next year. Wonderful news.

The following morning, breakfast eaten and a final hot shower before it was time to start heading back to Matang with the newbies. Along the way Tim took us to a Sunday market to stock up on Behavioural Enrichment goodies. I managed to get an interesting selection but there were no insects/mealworms unfortunately, which would have been ideal, natural treats for the animals. Back to Matang for coffee on my verandah and to settle the group into their biliks before Tim took them on an introductory tour around the centre and the trail of enclosures. This gave me a chance to catch up with Caroline and Keith, as Keith had now returned from his trip back to England. Daniel, his son had returned with him for a visit so it was lovely to meet him also. Once the others returned from the tour it was time for shopping and lunch in Matang Jaya til about 7.30pm then back to biliks for the remainder of the evening when all the volunteers came over to mine once more. It seems my verandah is the ideal meeting place, being larger than the others and with plenty of comfortable seating. We sat chatting on the verandah til 10.15 then it was off to bed ready for their first day at work tomorrow.

"We travel not to escape life, but for life not to escape us"

Anon

CHAPTER TEN

"A mind that is stretched by a new experience can never go back to its old dimensions"

Oliver Wendell Holmes

Well, the new group of volunteers turned up bright and eager for their first day at work, all kitted out in safari gear and straw hats! It looked like a scene from 'It ain't 'alf hot mum' a comedy series on TV from the 70s. I had to smile bless 'em but then again that sort of material is ideal for the humidity and actually a lot cooler than my scruffy shorts and t-shirts I wear. They were all enthusiastic so that was a great start. One of the men, Gary, was a very tall man, around 6'3", but we soon discovered he did seem to scream at any little thing, such as spiders, which was very funny coming from such a big chap. I do get the impression they all seem a bit keen on drinking – we shall see.

Today was also a good day as for the first time I received letters from home – it was absolutely lovely reading them and felt like my partner and my mum were there with me. Keith and Caroline both have an opportunity to work for Dr Alison Cronin, either in Dorset (Monkey

World) or Vietnam (Dao Tien). Before making a decision they have been invited to visit the rescue centre in Vietnam for a couple of days at the end of the month, to see what its about. As Heather has now returned home to the UK, Caroline asked if I would mind looking after Ting San whilst they were away, as long as this was approved by Tim. Of course I would need to spend time with her beforehand to thoroughly understand her routine and requirements, as well as ensuring Ting San was happy with me. Oooh, difficult decision – NOT! Of course I jumped at the chance and felt extremely privileged. Needless to say, this meant another day where I was drifting around in an amazing world of excitement and possibility racing through my brain.

After work Karen and Sally were eager to be shown the way to the river, where we could enjoy a wonderful cool down and respite from the heat. I quickly changed and as I was locking up only then did I remember that I would also need a towel. Now for the dilemma. All of this time I had religiously taken off my shoes before entering any building but I had just laced up my boots, the girls were waiting and I needed to get back in for my towel.

It was JUST THERE! Literally 2 steps away. Would it count if I kept my shoes on and just tip-toed in those couple of steps to reach it?! I couldn't bring myself to do this however and dutifully bent down to unlace my boots again to retrieve my towel. Once we reached the river we were treated to a very strange beauty therapy session, one which would later become a huge fad around the world. Our treatment however was totally free, unforced and completely natural, being in harmony with the fish. I don't know what the fish species is called but they swarm around us in the water, nibbling gently at our skin, removing dead skin and leaving us feeling soft and smooth. The fish feel like they have little tiny teeth, a very bizarre feeling but also a very cool experience. Little crayfish type things were also swimming around and nipping at my fingers.

Returning back to the biliks, Karen kindly invited me over to dinner with her, Gary and Sally. She proceeded to make a lovely chicken curry, followed by actual Neopolitan Ice-Cream for dessert!. This was a huge surprise as nothing lasts 2 seconds in the heat out here, so how on earth ice-cream could remain intact was mind-blowing. It did have a bit of a plasticy taste to it and was a bit elastic as it melted, which was a tad worrying. Maybe it has heaps of unhealthy fat or worse, some kind of plastic product within its makeup. I later discovered chocolate bars had the same weird consistency and taste. Not particularly pleasant but I suppose they do the job if you are craving something along those lines when travelling. Each time I worked abroad I found my body actually craved tomatoes and strawberry milk!!! No idea why, particularly strawberry milk as I never drink it at home.

The following day we had a journalist from 'Ex-Pat' magazine arrive, talking to us about why we volunteer at Matang. Its good that they are getting local interest which will hopefully lead to people in the ex-pat community here actually coming to visit and maybe also volunteering. That would be so beneficial and therefore definitely worth a go.

Keith apparently sang my praises to Alison Cronin at Monkey World, telling her I am a great animal/primate keeper so that is high praise from Keith and maybe a possible link to a job at Monkey World or Dao Tien further down the line. That would be very interesting.

Also today I saw a stick insect that REALLY looked like a stick – well, more of a thick twig actually, it was amazing. The bugs here are so much more larger than life than anywhere I have seen before. Its like one of my favourite TV programmes of the 70s - 'Land of the Giants'.

As I suspected, Penny is really grating on me already – she comes across as thinking no-one but her has any common sense, or ideas worth hearing. She is only young, just out of Uni, so may calm down a bit and mature through the weeks! It must be hard to adjust to the real world after the type of institutionalised University way of life. Good to see enthusiasm though.

Most of my time today was spent concentrating on enrichment for the centre, Emily the gibbons' enclosure furniture and starting to document enrichment ideas and nutritional requirements for all the species here. Once completed I will be ready to hand these over to the centre staff as illustrated folders when I leave. This will help all local keepers to carry on what we have been doing thus far, to improve the standards of care and also for future volunteers to access as training manuals, hopefully maintaining and constantly building on it as time goes by.

    I managed to cook an OK meal for myself with rice, green vegetables, seaweed and quorn chicken style nuggets. Not a good enough standard to invite anyone to dinner yet, but I'm making progress slowly. Heather texted me to say it was very cold in England and I should imagine she did really feel it after her extensive stay here. Later, around 12.30am, I was awoken by another text from home and was then kept awake for most of the night by torrential rain, thunder and lightening. An extremely impressive storm but I would have preferred a bit of sleep really. The first storms I experienced here were dramatic and exciting but, after a while, it is surprising what becomes normal – and a little bit pesky when you are tired. My! I have been spoilt!

Following on from not much sleep, I was then a bit annoyed when a circular saw suddenly appeared from a locked cupboard to saw the wood we were using to build platforms etc. Oh how we struggled to saw this iron wood by hand before, sweating like crazy, when all the time a circular saw was sitting idle in a cupboard!!! It seems we can be trusted with power tools now that we have men in the group. Unbelievable. It was much harder work, needing 'manly muscles' if you like, to saw by hand than to use mamby-pamby power tools. Grrrrr!!!! Oh well, at least they are cracking on with the fencing Chris and Deb started! I managed to finish the press feeder for Emily's enclosure, so we are pretty much ready to kit her out now.

It was a hassle free afternoon where we could really get some work done and cracked on well, although Tim had to take Penny into Kuching with a suspected eye infection.

Caroline stayed at home to do office work so Keith took Ting San into the forest for the afternoon. Luckily, I fed the macaques on the hill later than usual as, while I was there, Ting San came bowling down the boardwalk towards me with no sign of Keith. She held her arms up, asking me to pick her up and carry her and so we set out to find him together. We soon came across him and I learned that apparently she had gone up into the trees and worked her way swiftly along, giving him the slip. She was being a typical toddler and wouldn't go back to him so I carried her back and put her to bed. She can be a proper little madam sometimes! She kept pushing Keith away with her knuckles but wanted to hold his hand all the way. Treat for me anyways! Joseph, the new orangutan keeper from Semenggoh, is apparently due to start work here at Matang next week. It really needs to be Monday if Ting San has any chance of getting to know him before Keith and Caroline go to Vietnam for 2 days or so to check out Dao Tien in Vietnam as a possible new assignment running another endangered species centre, although this will mean I will no longer have the opportunity to take care of her in the interim.

I cooked myself an OK dinner of bacon, egg, cheesy baked beans and leftover veg rice from yesterday. It actually went down a treat and then I was invited over to Sally, Karen and Gary's again for drinks and chocolate. They went and bought bottles of Gin today, having discovered the Ting & Ting supermarket in Kuching, which sells European delights including alcohol, chocolate, cans of escargot and many other items you would not expect to find here. This group seem to REALLY be fixated with alcohol! We played cards for a couple of hours and had a good evening then it was back home for a good nights sleep, fingers crossed.

It is day 38 and I am gonna swing for that girl – I've never had anyone grate on me quite as much as her, not even that bloke Mike that was here with the Orangutarians! I just really struggle with the type of personality that feels it has to offer opinions and advice in every sentence, ask ridiculous questions and always has to add their experiences to attempt to 'top trump' everyone's stories. Aaaagh!

All was forgotten at lunchtime however when my cat gave birth to her first kitten in front of me on the verandah – it was a breach and pretty big but she did it fine. So cool. I watched as she carried it off to my cardboard box of water bottles and then had to tear myself away to return to work. I couldn't help popping back and checking in on her an hour later. She had now produced 3 kittens – all suckling and content, reducing in size as they were born. The first was a tabby, followed by a white blotchy one and lastly another tabby. I immediately texted Leanne, Deb and Heather with the wonderful news, not even thinking of stopping to figure out the time difference, but I knew they wouldn't mind at all and would be as excited as I was.

Dunno which is worse after a hard days work – James' usual Malaysian music CD or his CD of Christmas Carols. How can the same songs be played over and over and over, every single day? Even the best music couldn't hold up to this much exposure favourably on a long term basis...... and carols – well in my mind they just don't fit into a tropical rainforest backdrop in Borneo – a totally bizarre experience! Added to this torture of the senses, my cooking has gone downhill again. I decided on a vegetarian-style mutton in a packet of randan sauce with seaweed stuff. It would have been absolutely great, but the sauce was WAAAY too hot for me, even after I added a whole carton of coconut milk AND a packet of coconut. I was hungry so picked out the 'meat' as best I could, but I just couldn't eat the rest. Instead I found a couple of Roti and a beer to ease it down!

Spending time with my cat and her kittens was just gorgeous – I'm not going to be quite so lonely of a night-time now. The others kindly gave me an open invitation to join them any time, but they're just not the same as the last group. Nice enough but ... I think the first month I was here was all new to me and I was adapting at the same pace as the first group, having arrived together. Whereas now, I feel part of the furniture and almost a member of staff, rather than a volunteer. Added to this sense of belonging I also realise my time will, inevitably, be coming to an end, so I need to crack on and achieve as much as I can before that day arrives, ensuring my Training Manuals are written, printed and in place, to carry on in my absence. I also appreciate my down time, digesting all my experiences and thoughts, trying to ensure I capture all I dreamed I would. I spent the evening with my MP3 player and headphones, really enjoying my music mix – the soundtrack to my experience, plus a couple of beers and, of course, my new feline family.

The following day was Friday and the rest of the group were going out to visit Semenggoh and the Fairy Caves as we had done the month before. Tim invited me along too but he also said I could go at any time in the future if I wanted to, which was lovely of him considering he had taken me to visit them already. I am happy that I have been to see them, and they were amazing, but I came here to work and that's my intention today. Well, I say work. It turned out to be an absolutely cracking day.

I spent the morning with Caroline and Ting San in the forest, with Ting San very relaxed and happy for me to be there. I got totally bitten and 'leeched' but I didn't care. Note to self - must wear long trousers next time! Caroline also pointed out some little tiny mushrooms as we walked around which apparently glow in the dark, and would be amazing to see. We returned to the centre for lunch as usual and were happily sitting outside in the cool tiled porch area at the side when Doris decided to escape her enclosure and come over to join us. It is so sad to see how she walks bi-pedally most of the time, standing upright and curling her feet round so she walks on the outer edge of both feet. Hopefully, with more rehabilitation she will one day learn more natural behaviours. It was great she was out though. As I said previously, Doris is a very humanized orangutan and a very gentle girl with it. She craves companionship, especially human companionship. Ting San was a little worried initially but they mainly ignored one another. Doris is very playful with Mamu but sensed that Ting San was a different character so left it to her to make the first moves. Talking of Mamu, she was the next to appear on our side of the bars, but didn't get to venture down and join us as Ciam, her mum, promptly yanked her back in!

It just so happened that the new baby orangutan training enclosure was finished this morning so Keith persuaded the head keepers to let Doris and Ting San go in and test it all out. They absolutely loved it. We all had a great afternoon – such a special "our time" moment for Keith, Caroline, me and Keith's son Daniel. Daniel was a joy to watch with Doris having grown up in the company of gorillas and other great apes as a child due to Keith's job history. Daniel was just so at ease and natural with her, helping her to explore the different apparatus around the enclosure quietly and gently, as another orang would have done.

Doris finished the day by climbing in to visit Tim and Simon, the Samber Deer, then having a go at climbing a tree, even though it was ever so slightly and she only managed the confidence to scale it a few feet. An excellent time was had by all, and the new nursery enclosure stood up to the girls' scrutiny with great aplomb.

That night we all returned to the Jambu restaurant for a meal and a quiz night. We came last in the quiz but Daniel regained the honour of the Matang posse by performing some of his songs for everyone. He is a very accomplished and well known busker in the UK and it was wonderful to see the pride in Keith's eyes as he watched, and joined in some of the songs with his son. A wonderful evening and Keith and Caroline invited me to stay over at their house with them, rather than return to Matang alone. It was the weekend and the rest of the group would be staying in Kuching so I accepted and we sat chatting until around 1.30am but were aware that we needed to be up again at 6.30am. I was told Joseph would be starting the beginning of next week, and he will be moving into my bilik with his family, meaning I will need to move over to Aqil's house next door. It was a bit of a surprise but I suppose it was inevitable. I had had the luxury of my own place for a while now, so had been very lucky and very privileged.

It was Saturday and Keith, Caroline and I were working. I de-frosted and cleaned out the enrichment food freezer, getting rid of things that had been lurking at the bottom that were goodness knows what and had been there for goodness knows how long. It was all clean and sparkling and then refilled with lots of fresh new stuff. Caroline hadn't finished all her lunch so donated her sandwiches for use in something. Well it was the worst combination I had ever heard of so far I think – Peanut Butter and Marmite!! Mind you maybe Caroline was ahead of her time because Sweet and Salt are now a very popular combination, with my favourite chocolate bar flavour being sea salt – maybe I should have given it a go back then but at the time it sounded particularly awful and I couldn't bring myself to try it.

Finishing my work for the day I noticed Jo, one of the Sun Bears has an amazing trick of rolling a tiny ball of saliva all around her body – how it keeps a perfect and constant pea-size sphere I don't know – totally bizarre but fascinating to watch and therefore a behaviour which likely takes her to a calm and relaxed place in her mind. It will be so good to get the bear enclosure completed so she will be able to find much more natural and fulfilling ways to spend her time and enjoy her days as a Sun Bear should. It can't come soon enough.

In the evening it was a second visit to the Longhouse at Kampong Rayu village. Each months group is invited to spend the evening with the centres workers, their families and neighbours. This one was hosted by John and his wife and was extra special, being Keith and Caroline's last one. On arrival we noticed the corridor had been decorated with batik wall hangings and a wedding tree took pride of place in the centre of the floor. This had a base post covered in hibiscus flowers and then plaited palms and other leaves spread out across the top as branches. Tied in the 'branches' were bottles of beer, peanuts in their shells, balloons and other items – probably representing food, drink, happiness and wealth to always be plentiful for the newly married couple. Rita did speeches and Keith and Caroline were given lots of presents by different people. Many were hand made items, very personal to both the giver and to Keith and Caroline, showing just how much the keepers and their families had grown to love them both during their time here.

The drink with our meal was not squash this time but milk, mixed with cherry cordial. It was quite nice but did look a lot like Peptobismol! The prepared feast of food was gorgeous with chicken dishes, fish, wild boar, rice, baby ferns, ground tapioca leaves etc. After dinner had been enjoyed by all and the speeches and gifts had finished, we were then treated to a re-enactment of a traditional Iban wedding. The women elders beat their drums and gongs and called at the house of the groom. The groom and the women then went to collect the bride from her house. The couple were then seated in front of the batik backdrop and the women played music whilst an older lady chopped ginger (or something) and cut a fruit (lime sized) into pieces. The pieces were tossed into the air and, dependent on how they landed, signified the sex of their first child. Face down a girl, face up a boy I think. A healthy white cockerel was also banded about, then taken away, I don't know what fate belied it, or what significance to the ceremony it held. The young 'bride to be' performed the hornbill dance for us, which was absolutely mesmerising again. Once the wedding ceremony had been conducted we were treated to a second dance. This time it was to be performed by the welder from the animal centre, proudly performing his dance, telling a traditional story through his movements, and his own personal story through the depictions on his heavily tattooed body. He was dressed in his ceremonial loin cloth or *cawat* (with shorts underneath), a colourful red embroidered tabbard and a gold coloured headpiece. As the women started to play he began his particular warrior dance. There are several warrior dances, known as *Ngajat* which would likely have been performed when warriors returned home from battles. The movements are slow, to symbolise stalking the enemy, with moments of leaping and dramatic movements to symbolise moving forward to attack. His performance was so understated yet so powerful and moving. Again, we were transfixed as he wove his story using carefully choreographed movements, no doubt handed down through generations. He is an elderly man but danced well, his traditional Iban tattoos all over his body, detailing his own personal history and story. That is why I love traditional tattoos so much. They tell your story, they are not just a heart or a row of stars, or love and hate on your knuckles – these are the origin of tattoos, the reason of tattoos and they are worn with pride and honour.

I didn't see the little girl down the road this time and wondered how she was doing. This time, I felt sorry for Tim – he had driven us all to the Longhouse but then settled down on the floor in the corridor and worked on his laptop all evening, before driving us home again at the end of the night. Work never stops when you are responsible for running a project as large as this.

It really was a great night, so much work and preparation had gone into making it such a spectacular traditional celebration and evening for us all. The Tuak and Lancow seemed much stronger this time and was free-flowing, tons of it! Beer was also passed around aplenty. Sadly, Cora was unwell so hadn't been able to come with us this evening, the only chance she will probably get to visit a longhouse community. Such a shame for her. We danced together for the rest of the night, Keith and Daniel singing again and then, on returning home to 'the street', most of the volunteers finished up at mine, drinking on the verandah until nearly 4 o'clock in the morning, when I was suddenly totally wrecked and had to crash for a few hours sleep. I am so glad I have tomorrow off. I noticed Penny and Daniel disappeared off together and, as she had done at the longhouse, Karen continued to rip small strips from her skirt, handing the strips out to anyone that would take it and tying pieces on to some of the boys. Maybe a piece of her skirt had ripped at the longhouse and she had fiddled with it. Then, like a ripped piece of wallpaper on a peeling wall, she just couldn't leave it alone, ripping more and more bits off. Or maybe she felt like a rock star, treating her adoring fans to a small piece of her stage costume. I don't know, quite a bizarre thing to do, but she was enjoying herself immensely and when you are happy, and tiddly, it is surprising what you find entertaining sometimes!

Before heading to bed I set the alarm clock, just in case Keith didn't wake as he was crashing at mine and, unlucky for him, he WAS working the next day. Lucky I did, he was sound asleep bless him. I eventually managed to stir him and then discovered we had been locked in and Mum cat was locked out! Bit of a panic whilst wondering who would have locked my door as they left the night before, and why?! Also worried about the kittens and mum cat being stressed, not being able to reach them. This predicament threw me for a while, as I was feeling really rather rough, but then I suddenly came to my senses and remembered that ALL the windows are actually French doors, so I merely moved along to the next set, 'et voila', they of course were not locked and we were free once more. Disaster averted and Keith was able to get off to work. I threw up in a bucket, had an Ibuprofen and a drink of water and then returned to bed to try to sleep again.

"Travel makes one modest, you see what a tiny place you occupy in the world"

Gustave Flaubert

CHAPTER ELEVEN

"People don't take trips – trips take people"
John Steinbeck

I managed to get some sleep and woke up at 12.20pm feeling a lot better, although certainly not 100%. It was a really hot and sunny day so an ideal day to set to and do my washing before heading to the centre to check that Keith and Daniel were OK at work looking after Ting San. They were absolutely fine, and James' wife, Leah, and the kids had joined them, playing with Ting San. I fed all the macaques and then returned home to relax for the rest of the day. The others all popped in for chats early in the evening but then I had a quiet night to ensure I was fit and well for work the following day.

The next morning I still wasn't 100% but OK enough. I had a good incentive to crack on as it turned out to be a really worthwhile and productive day today. Aaron, Cora and myself actually got to furnish Emily the gibbon's enclosure. We did a good job I reckon. We watched as she explored the extreme makeover. She had never had movement in her furnishings before, something which is crucial to any primate enclosure as it replicates movement they would encounter in a natural environment of tree canopies, branches and leaves. Emily didn't know what to make of it initially so she proceeded to step around everything, continuing to use the bars of her cage to get around, but she was definitely intrigued and slowly began to test out the moving objects, one foot or one hand at a time. She also seemed to be relishing winding up her neighbours, the pig-tailed macaques, as they appear to be so very jealous. Your turn next guys, I promise.

As we were working on Emily's enclosure, James came around with some local visitors. They were looking to donate 3 pig-tailed macaques to Matang. It turns out the macaques live with an elderly relative of theirs who is dying, so they will need to rehome the macaques as soon as possible. The visitors obviously care for them and want them to have as decent a captive life as possible. They seemed impressed with the work we were doing which of course then made James proud and eager for us to furnish the macaque enclosure too. It is full steam ahead. Some serious discussion needs to take place beforehand though as I don't know how they will be able to integrate 3 new macaques into the current troop, with the facilities that we have – furnished or unfurnished.

Penny went off at lunchtime to spend time with Daniel before he leaves to return to the UK. In the evening Sally, Karen and Gary invited us all over for dinner at theirs. We were also joined by Graham, a visiting Australian Sound Ecologist we had met at Singgahsana previously. He was very interested in Matang so had come to visit and have a look around.

Returning to my Bilik I decided to defrost the icebox in my fridge, so I could actually get stuff in it that was larger than a CD case! Once defrosted I could also then refit the broken off icebox door, which was the cause of the severe frostiness, ensuring it was all nice and clean and ready for Joseph and his family to move in. Unfortunately, breaking all the golden rules of defrosting freezers, I had no plastic scrapers or anything similar so I resorted to a knife to stab away at the last remnants of ice. In my haste to finish the job and get to bed, I stabbed the side a little too enthusiastically, puncturing the inner wall and so releasing all the gas (HFC I believe) into the atmosphere. Not the best action of an environmentally conscious volunteer in a rainforest in Borneo. I have now killed my freezer box and probably the whole fridge to boot too! Whoops!!

The following day Tim brought Joseph and his family to check out the centre and my house. They all liked what they saw and the job was duly accepted, he will start next Monday and therefore move in at the weekend. The fridge is completely broken so I am hoping the centre will be able to find another to replace it before the family arrive. I will be moving into Aqils house next door, and Aqil will be part-commuting from his family home and part staying on-site in the backpackers longhouse until I finish my volunteering. I offered to move in with Aaron and Cora, if Penny went in with Aqil but Aqil is OK with the arrangement as it stands. This means I will continue to have my own space, although I feel bad that Aqil will be leaving his own home to accommodate me.

That afternoon Aqil kindly drove all the volunteers around different shops in the local area, in order for us to stock up on food. First stop, surprise surprise, saw us having to drive all the way to Kuching (45 minutes each way) just so the others could go to Ting & Ting supermarket for Gin, Vodka and Wine! Then it was back towards Matang, stopping en route first at Everrise supermarket for vegetarian/vegan supplies such as mock duck, then to the usual supermarket, Choice Ria, for fruit and vegetables. The last stop was just outside the gates of the centre, where we could buy beer. Some of them are doing my head in a bit now, but I treated them to a big cake anyway, as they have been very good to me – cooking, shopping, buying cat food, helping furnish Emily gibbon etc. They invited me round in the evening but really don't want to socialise with incessant drinking and annoying bouts of laughter. I just can't deal with noise, night after night. I thanked them all very much and drowned them out with my headphones, settling down to a relaxing game of patience with my trusty pack of cards. This was my best way of relaxing in the evenings during the latter part of my time here. I really think the volunteers are being unfair to the families living in the street, especially as the children need to be up for school so early in the mornings. I am going to hear it even more when I move opposite them at the weekend! At least they will be off to Bako National Park for a couple of days so I can settle in peacefully to start me off. I think the main thing that has got to me is noticing that Gary and Karen are spending less and less time at the centre actually volunteering and working and more time in their bilik relaxing and drinking. They did say that this is a holiday and they want to enjoy themselves but I understand they will be travelling for 6 months in all, so 4 weeks working in a centre, helping animals, surely isn't too much to ask. They have paid for their place here though, as we all have, so at least the centre isn't losing out financially, just losing a little manpower.

Keith gave me some Crocodile teeth, porcupine quills and pheasant feathers to take back as gifts for my fellow workers back at Woburn, who I know will absolutely be chuffed to bits. They all love wildlife so much and were instrumental in the making of my totem necklace, it will be fantastic to be able to return with totems from Borneo for them. Perfect, and a good job the UK was not as strict as Australia with regards customs and what can be brought into the country, at that time anyway, it is probably much stricter now.

I tended to give myself space from the others at work the following day too. Getting the go ahead with James to convert an overgrown aviary, next to the chickens, for Thea the cockatoo, after he assured me the chickens would not be a disease risk, I asked Aqil to organise some of the volunteers to clear, clean and furnish the enclosure while I went 'foraging for perches'. This gave me a perfect opportunity to disappear off and spend an hour or so with Caroline and Ting San, whilst 'foraging for perches'!

Keith and Daniel were going into Kuching to have tattoos done today. Sadly they couldn't get hold of Ernesto so are going to an alternative, cheaper place they have found. They are both having a picture of Ting San, drawn from a photo by Keith. Keith is an amazing artist and actually also designed the T-shirts for Matang volunteers, which have a stunning drawing of Aman the Orangutan on them.

I quietly did the behavioural enrichment rounds to the different animals on my own and then set to preparing enrichment ready for the next day. I also managed to do this alone, apart from a little interference from Penny. Having had a wonderfully peaceful day up to now, and nearly making it to the end of our working day unhindered, I'm afraid I lost my rag and swore at her, although I did immediately apologise as this is not like me and not fair on her, she is totally oblivious to social skills sometimes so not really her fault – oops!

Apparently the 2 Samba Deer who share the large enclosure with Doris the orangutan have now become aggressive so the volunteers won't be able to go in with her. It may be a seasonal change in behaviour but at the moment it would be unsafe. They do seem fine with Doris, especially as, being an orangutan she spends most of her time up high on platforms anyway. It is a little sad for the volunteers and Caroline considered offering them all a one-to-one with Ting San to make up for it but they do all get to be with her in the mornings on the patio every day, and never seem to take many photos or much notice of her really, so we decided between us to leave it.

Come the end of the working day, I was really frustrated, annoyed, and saddened. I discovered that the Cockatoo had been moved into her new aviary but had been provided with no rounded branches to perch on - despite me bringing some good ones back from the forest. The people doing it then casually mentioned to me in passing that one of the chickens was slowly dying, and that the others were pecking at it. For goodnesses sake – don't just watch, do nothing, and let it suffer!! Caroline rescued it, James dispatched of it and chopped it up for the bears. Sadly though Corinne never got any for some reason, poor little girl. Maybe James miscalculated the amount of pieces he needed.

Keith and I did the Cockatoo enclosure properly by including perches, toys, food, water, bath and substrates of sand and stones. I am much happier with it now.

That evening I think it must have been payback time for the noise made by the volunteers because, just to top of my not so great day, there was a full blast music battle going on in the street. James was playing his usual local music CD, interspersed with nursery rhymes and Christmas Carols, whereas the family in the end house were playing thrash metal!! Woahhh!! This went on for quite a while but, in the end, the Carols won out.

At work the next day James confirmed to us that we would be getting the 3 female pigtail macaques from the family who visited recently. We all joined forces to rig out the middle pen of the macaques on the hill in readiness. James, Aaron and Keith put in the base wooden structures to build on, then Cora and I started putting in ropes and furnishings. Its looking good, and the macaque boys got additional enrichment being able to watch us build it all, although it wasn't finished yet so we kept them shut off from this part of the enclosure for now. Aaron and Cora, are both so enthusiastic at work and a pleasure to be with. They both would have fitted in well with the last group too.

In a much happier frame of mind, having achieved more suitable surroundings for differing animals, I invited everyone round to mine in the evening. Karen had shown Aqil how to cook Spaghetti Bolognese for everyone, so we all tucked in with an accompaniment of some wine and beer, Manu Chiao playing in the background and a card game of Happy Families (hahaha)!!! It was really nice actually, not drunken and rowdy just pleasant and relaxed. As you may have noticed I had invited everyone round but hadn't actually cooked myself, I wouldn't have put that on anyone.

Aaron, Cora and I finished furnishing the middle macaque enclosure the following day. They were spellbound, watching intently all morning as we toiled away. Finally finishing just before midday we could let them through into their new, improved home. Well, I nearly cried, Cora did cry – they were like kids in a toy store at Xmas. It was fantastic to watch. They swung, pushed, pulled, climbed, jumped and bounded, testing and sampling everything in there. Even swimming in the cleaned out water trough. They were soooo happy bless them, from having absolutely nothing in there to a complete floor to ceiling assault course with gadgets and gizmos. Awesome.

We started the second enclosure in the afternoon, wanting to really move this on now, as the 3 new pigtails were coming from the private owner sometime very soon and the more facilities available in the enclosure, the less likely they are to have issues when integrating, with plenty of areas to retreat to and plenty of options on ways to travel around the enclosure. It is now a fully functional 3D space.

The others finished work at lunchtime to go to Singgahsana, ready for their weekend in Bako tomorrow. Cora and Aaron however, wanted to stay on and work on the enclosures with us, so Keith and Caroline drove them in later. They are a really good couple who both truly appreciate the role of volunteering and have the compassion to give it their all. Wonderful people.

After work I moved in to Aqil's house and he moved out. I feel really bad about it but he says he is quite happy about the situation and I must admit it is nice to have a homely place with a proper lounge, complete with sofa, armchair, coffee table and window coverings. Not to mention a power shower and a fridge that works! I made myself very comfortable indeed. I plumped for the small single bedroom as it is out the back, so should be a little quieter, and has an air-con fan, whereas the double bedroom in the front of house has no curtains and no fan. I had to give it a good clean under my bed and scrubbed the whole shower room, as it was thick with grime, but a small price to pay for such a lovely home.

I actually also achieved making myself a good dinner and put a load of washing in to soak and wash later. However, only then did I notice there was no washing line though so I will have to drape my clean washing around the verandah as best I can when its done. Once all my tasks were complete I celebrated by laying on the sofa relaxing, with the French doors open, hoping to catch a small breeze, and complete and utter silence - as all the others are away, volunteers off to Bako for the weekend and local families having returned to their village homes for the weekend. Absolute bliss. However, little did I know what the following day would bring!!

"The man who goes alone can start today, but he who travels with another must wait til that other is ready"

Henry David Thoreau

CHAPTER TWELVE

*"All journeys have secret destinations of which the
traveller is unaware"*

Martin Buber

It was Saturday once more so Keith and I worked, giving Caroline a much needed day off. We spent the morning on the first platform with Ting San who was happily playing high up in the trees, coming back for a cuddle time with Keith a couple of times and a play with me. However, starting back down the trail towards the centre about 11.30, ready for Ting Sans lunch, we heard a lot of commotion at the pig-tailed macaques. I went to investigate and couldn't believe it – there were the 3 macaques we were planning to visit, do a preliminary health check on and then arrange transfer from the private owner. It was a mother and her 2 daughters, who had been clearly darted and were out cold, unconscious, laying on nothing more than pieces of cardboard in the concrete shut-off of the cage we were doing up. This shut off area is not secure so I was very concerned they would start to come round and climb up high, which is a natural instinct to escape danger in the wild when feeling vulnerable. If they did this they could then fall flat onto the concrete below. Unbelievable.

I was not a happy bunny. They must've known they were coming and therefore could've told us so we could do more to the enclosure to prepare and secure it properly. Before integrating any animals you must first check that they have no transferable diseases as a basic first step. Secondly, ensure they are healthy and able to cope with integration and then a careful plan must be put into place to integrate them into the current troop under careful supervision.

Instead, here were 3 lifeless primates, supposedly being rescued to a much better life, dumped into an unfinished home, which could have been stunning if they'd just waited half a day. The other macaques, who were making all the noise, were clearly upset with this unexpected arrival of seemingly dead fellow primates. Total confusion, stress and chaos. No-one who had transported these poor girls had hung around to see if they recovered from the sedation OK. Transporting unconscious animals is not good anyway but they were so heavily sedated, I was fearful of brain damage. I stayed with them, how could I leave them like this? Someone needed to care for them. How could I go to lunch and leave them like the vet obviously had. Lunch is a 2 hour affair here and so much could happen in that time. Very dangerous and uncaring practice. I was surprised.

The first of them started to come round and regain consciousness after about an hour. Ridiculous amount of time. Dread to think how long they had been sedated before arriving here. She was, not surprisingly, totally disorientated and doped up to the eyeballs. As predicted, her first hazy instinct was to climb and so she proceeded to climb to the top of the 20+ feet enclosure and cling to the wire mesh. The next one didn't start to come round for another HOUR after that. Insane. The Mum was concerning me as there was still no movement, no reactions, no blinking, no anything from her. There was still no-one else around and I was not going to leave these girls. Luckily I had my phone on me so I texted Keith (who had Ting San to deal with) and told him she was not good, her breathing becoming shallower by the minute. There was a real fear we were going to lose her. But, there was nothing we could do until James returned to the centre from his lunch at 2pm. Keith managed to come up and join me to assess her then. He asked if I was happy to stay with her and to keep poking her with a stick through the bars to keep her moving as best I could until help arrived. If I could have opened that enclosure space I would have, to grab that little girl and get some help for her. But that wasn't an option so there was I, sobbing, poking this poor macaque with a stick, close to death. I was pleading with her to hang on a little longer, and a little longer. By this time it was raining, torrential rain. She was lying on her side, drowning in this rain and still couldn't move or respond to save herself. I couldn't have been any wetter, my tears lost in the rain pouring down on me. Eventually, after what seemed a lifetime, James came to see but didn't actually know what she'd been given anaesthetic wise. He then had to call the previous owners to get the number of the vet and call him! I have never been more frustrated and experience time go so slowly. Eventually, about 2.30pm the vet was on the way. This had been 3 hours, with at least another hour in capture and transit. It will all probably be too late, I can't keep her going this way. Keith then thankfully took the decision to risk getting in and grabbing her, to get her to the vet room and rub her as dry as he could in an attempt to raise her core temperature. He and the head keeper did that, risking bites from her if she came round, and also attacks from her frightened (and un-health checked) daughters. It was the only way.

Luckily, Ting San was happy to go into the forest with me for the afternoon, leaving Keith free to save mum macaque. It was just what I needed actually to calm me down and make me smile again.

Still soaking wet and not a cup of tea or coffee, let alone food, but I was oblivious. Ting San was so loving and we were like a couple of mates. She would put her arms up for me to carry her, or take my hand and lead me down the trail. Her body language is so clear as to what she wants of you. If you stop at a tree she doesn't want to climb she pushes away from it with her knuckles. If she wants you to show her something or repeat an action she takes your hands and places them down onto what she wants you to do. She spent ages with me on a little wooden bridge over a small stream, making me pick up leaves and gather water for her by folding them. She also spent ages trying to get me to climb a tree after her, by putting my hands on the trunk, climbing part way, then holding her hand out towards me, to follow. When I didn't, or more to the point couldn't, she climbed down again, took my hand and pulled to try to get me climbing. Time and time again she tried but eventually figured I'm a rubbish playmate so we made our way back to meet Keith and put her to bed at 4pm. The Vet had eventually arrived and given mum (now known as 'Dodd') a reversal drug – she had been completely overdosed bless her. The family also returned, which was nice and showed their care, also meaning Keith could then ask what their names were (always helpful to settle them in!) and what food they were used to so we didn't upset their metabolism. The last thing they needed on top of everything else would be an upset stomach. It is imperative that you learn as much as you can about any animals' background in order to make their transition as easy and stress free as possible.

Dodd is apparently 12 years old and her daughters are Tammy and Baby. Dodd was now in a small cage to recover in the Kitchen – her breathing had improved and she was blinking so hopefully she'll make it. What a terrible time she's having.

Getting home for a shower and to put some dry clothes on at last, I discovered a leech on each of my ankles. I was so mentally exhausted I decided to just let them have their fill so they would then drop off naturally. However, neither wound would stop bleeding. I was of the understanding that leeches sealed up the wounds after they had gorged themselves, but they clearly hadn't done this. There's gratitude for you!

Once I was clean and dry again, I was feeling half-human. I received a text from my Mum, which was cool at the end of such a traumatic day, but sadly learned that Aunt Shirl had passed away so Mum and Dad had been keeping a check on Aunt Bet and would be going to the funeral.

Next up I finished the load of washing I had started yesterday but, unfortunately my pyjamas had run, so now I have navy blue streaks on absolutely everything! Sort of a tie-dye effect but not quite enough to get away with it or to look anything but awful. Oh well, they'll have to do for working in!

Last thing on the agenda before calling it a night, I wanted to return to the centre and check on Dodd and the girls' progress and also Emily the gibbon, as she was next to the macaques and must have felt the tension and stress of the day also. She made my world good again as I couldn't help but laugh to see that she had settled for the night ON TOP of her lovely new house, rather than it it! Bless her, she looked so content and I loved her that little bit more. She gurgles and grunts when I scratch her belly through the mesh.

James was not at the centre so I returned to the street to wait for him to return home from where ever he was. However, I could hear announcements from a distance away so I came to the conclusion that there must be something going on at the Longhouse. It got to 8.45pm and still no-one had arrived back so I decided to go it alone to check on Dodd, with the only torch I had, my trusty Netto's head torch! I had no keys and couldn't go through the orangutan gates or I would wake Ting San up, so I decided to try and find a back way I had discovered when caring for Ting San earlier today. I only had sandals to wear as my boots were like sunken boats from the ordeal in the rain today. It was a bit of a risk in the forest in the dark but "Hey ho", needs must. I was a bit worried and trod as carefully as I could, making it safely through to the lookout tower at the back of the new bear enclosure. I was hoping to find the glow in the dark mushrooms along the way. Sadly, I didn't. Also, rather unfortunately, I discovered there was no path round the side to come up behind Quarantine. Retracing my steps I then had to make my way back through the forest safely and walk round to the front. All fences and gates had barbed wire across the top, except our green gate leading to the centres patio area. I found it easy to climb over, even in sandals, giggling quietly to myself that I must've looked like something out of Mission Impossible!

I found Dodd was sitting up and responding to her name, although still groggy. She had however managed to pull all the covers off her cage so was sitting there in the bright glare of the fluorescent lights in the kitchen.

Luckily the door had broken earlier today so it was not lockable, only the outer mesh door. This meant I could reach my arm through the open kitchen door, talk to her and then switch the light off so she could get some respite and rest. She should be OK until the morning. Climbing back over the gate I returned home from my mission rather pleased with myself!

Dodd was much more alert the next morning but her eyelids are still not functioning properly. We decided to keep her back today, just in case, due to her being groggy and likelihood of falling if in a big high cage. She seems to be a very gentle and calm girl but I don't know if the drugs have caused any permanent damage. They now reckon she was given a full syringe, which is at least 5ml and enough to knock an orangutan out. Ludicrous. The owners came back to visit her again and said they will also be back tomorrow. The other 2 are not eating and seem, naturally, very anxious at the moment without their mum. We need to get them back together as soon as possible. Additionally, we wondered how Dodd would react with Juan, a very young pig-tailed macaque who came in alone. It may be worth a one-to-one to see how he would react to a potential surrogate mother. It may just be an ideal chance to get him into some kind of stable mind and become part of a family.

Out with Keith and Ting San on the forest platforms all morning I got bitten to pieces by mosquitos. I have learned that the black and white ones are the worst for bites – they really itch! Ting San has now decided she will not go anywhere without me and I have to carry her. She still goes to Keith for cuddles and then me for transportation. I always knew I had child-bearing hips but didn't realise they were there to someday be mum to an orange baby with mad hair! Personally, this is much preferred to raising children!!

Tim the deer escaped twice during the afternoon, deciding he wanted to explore further afield. I, meanwhile, took Ting San into the newly built orphan enclosure for a while where she had great fun playing in the little pool, doing angels on her back with her arms and legs as if she was in some imaginary snowdrift, kicking out at the water and getting absolutely drenched with a goofy, happy expression on her face. Happily I caught it on video and have since posted this on YouTube (Orangutan Angel). Excellent. If you watch it please forgive the annoying whooping noises of a passing visitor to the centre.

Penny and Sally came back to the biliks following their weekend away but the two couples decided to take an extra night in Singgahsana. This was fine as it meant the 3 of us all had a house each! Very decadent. I phoned my partner, and actually got through after 3 frustrating weeks of failure to connect. However, it went to the answering machine – she's probably still in bed! Ho hum.

As arranged Joseph started at Matang that Monday to take over orangutan rehabilitation, starting with Ting San. It must be really hard for Caroline to hand over and prepare to walk away, having initially rescued her and raised her. I know how this little bundle of fun has affected me after just a handful of times I've been with her. It is best for her though, and to think one day she could be living free, having babies of her own, that's what its all about. Joseph says she has been spoilt by being carried to and from the forest, and thinks she should walk the whole way on her own. It seems a bit harsh as a 2½ year old would still be clinging to Mum in the wild, but he is very good with orangs and she seems to have taken to him very quickly.

Leaving her in his more than capable hands we set off and visited the house where the 3 macaques came from in Kampong Selang. Very nice houses but we came to learn not such nice people living in them! We drove past a house set on the corner of the road, with two palm trees outside. One had a recently burnt bonfire against it, the other had a cross beam attached with two long-tailed macaques chained by the neck. Apparently the older one (with an eye missing and a crooked neck) was alone for a long time but now has a friend in the form of a baby (approx 6-9 months old). Both males. Keith took photos to inform IPPL, WSPA, SFC and anyone else who may be able to help them, with a view to trying to persuade the 'owners' to hand them over in the future.

They played on my mind and I later told Gavin, as he and SFC may be able to check whether they have a license and intervene quite quickly. At the least the 3 macaques had been loved and cared for of sorts in a large cage, approx 12' high and 8' square. It had a couple of shelves and a protective roof so they had shelter and a place to rest.

The lady who handed over the girls is called Diana and was the sister of the chap that lived there. She is a real animal lover, living in Kuching with 40 cats and 15 dogs apparently, plus she had just picked up 5 puppies from the middle of the road. She shuts them all in the house when she goes out as she doesn't trust people not to harm them. I cannot begin to imagine 60 dogs and cats shut in one house, or even living there with freedom to roam. I wonder if she has neighbours close by!

Apparently her brother also had the male (father) macaque until about a year ago but some friendly neighbours decided to kill him by thrusting an iron bar into him. Also she told us her brother laying collapsed in his house and neighbours came in and robbed him of his gold necklace, bracelet and ring as he lay there. They didn't even call for help. She and her friend Harry had been busy clearing all remaining possessions from the house before they too were stolen. Her brother since died in hospital but she believes that the spirit remains for 7 days after death and said she definitely felt his warm presence in the house but was too frightened to stay there so had to clear it out before the 7 days had passed.

Harry her friend is a short man, with hair like Charlie Drake and he was wearing nail varnish. Funny little chap.

We agreed to return Wednesday and dismantle the cage and also agreed to try to help catch 2 chickens and an injured mum cat that was hanging around.

In the evening I attempted to make papier mache forage boards for the primates as an enrichment. This had failed on my first attempt as the 'glue' didn't dry off in the humidity, leaving me with a soggy mess of nothing. The idea is to spread little piles of nuts, seeds, dry fruit etc around a large piece of plywood (or similar). You would then use flour and water to 'glue' pieces of paper over the little piles which would then dry and take ages for little fingers to pick away at the paper to gain access to the treats hidden beneath. A great idea which keeps them entertained for hours but may not be a transferable enrichment idea in a Bornean rainforest environment. Gavin popped in to borrow my kettle for the next batch of "essentials" who were staying in the onsite longhouse accommodation overnight. We sat chatting for a while before Penny skulked over to join in. I could have swung for her a second time because, as Gavin left, he spotted his trainers and said "Ooh, there's my trainers, thought I'd lost them". Before I could then say I had been using them, she pipes up "Oh, are they your trainers?" She is just so oblivious to social etiquette or feeling she didn't stop there as any normal person might, instead she carried on "but haven't I seen you wearing them Marcia?" Lots of awkwardness followed for both myself and Gavin.

Amazing insects

Cultural Village Show

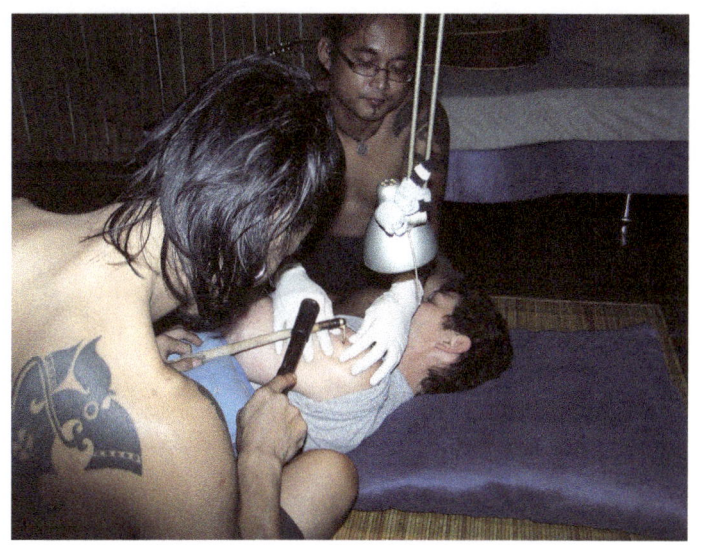

Getting my traditional tattoo done

Bear quarantine enclosure

"Not all those who wander are lost"

J R R Tolkien

CHAPTER THIRTEEN

*"Once you have travelled, the voyage never ends, but is
played out over and over again in the quietest
Chambers. The mind can never break off from the
journey"*

Pat Conroy

Kevin the pig-tailed macaque has a bad left wrist this
morning. He probably sprained it in a conflict over
food with Oliver. We will have to monitor his wrist, and
the situation. When we first arrived here Oliver was in a
separate section of the enclosure to Kevin and Chick but
since refurbishing the enclosure the boys are now
combined in one section so hierarchies are being tested.
Kevin used to dominate Chick and give him a hard time
but now he has found himself in the same boat, with him
now being dominated by Oliver. At least with new
furnishings in the enclosure he has platforms to rest on
now and places to avoid conflict, rather than either
clinging to the mesh with a bad wrist or sitting on the
cold, wet concrete floor below. Hopefully, once they
have sorted themselves out, they will be able to integrate
with the 3 new girls more calmly.

Gavin took us shopping in the afternoon which gave me a chance to catch up on emails. I only had a half hour slot on the computer so by the time I had sent a quick group email to everyone and deleted 60-odd rubbish emails, I only had time to read 4 that I had received from friends and family, including 2 from last months volunteers. In the evening I phoned my partner and actually managed to get hold of her before she headed out to the hospital for a kidney scan. She was a little frosty to begin with and this is when I learned I'd had a letter from the Kuching Hilton that had worried her. Apparently she wasn't aware I had stayed there with Deb (she had not been seeing the emails and I had been unable to reach her by phone). She had therefore put 2 and 2 together and thought the worst of me! Didn't help the fact they'd charged me additionally for the mini bar in the room (which they didn't have) so I must admit it did look rather suspect. It turned out they actually meant tea and coffee making facilities, which are normally free in any other hotel. The worst of it was we didn't even use the hotels tea and coffee sachets as it was Peppermint Tea, and Nescafe coffee (not supporting Nestle is a personal ethical stance), so we had bought our own teabags from the 7-eleven supermarket and only taken all their packets as souvenirs! An extra RM32 (about £5.80 in today's money) that cost me!! Cheek of it!

Keith, Aaron, Cora and I spent the following day dismantling the donated macaque cage at the house in Kampong Salang. It was very well built and ideal for use at the centre, but it was also secured in a foot of concrete! It was hard work and we got bitten to death by mosi's again for our troubles. Harry said he had seen a long tailed macaque in a nearby tree earlier in the day, so this maybe explains the ease of how people catch them for pets, like the two chained by the necks on the corner.

They come too near to houses for food, opportunistically stealing goodies through open doorways and windows. In most cases of captive baby animals the mother will be killed in order to take the baby, as any wild mother will protect her baby at all costs. James said nothing can be done about them as long-tailed macaques are not a protected species so there is no license needed to keep them as pets. Pig-tailed macaques are, however, protected. The only way we could free the two captive macaques on the corner, or any others we may come across, is if the owners could be persuaded to hand them over voluntarily.

We chatted with Diana as we worked on the cage and found her young daughter loves painting Diana's nails while she sleeps. This could maybe explain why Harry is wearing nail varnish then!

It took all day but we eventually managed to dismantle the enclosure, although we had no transport to bring it back to the centre as yet. The 3 macaque girls are settling in well now, and coming down to us for food which is great. Dodd is also looking quite normal now which is a huge relief.

Talking to Caroline later she told me that whilst they were out in the forest today Ting San had found a large shell, which she kept dipping into the little stream to fill with water and drink from. When she put the shell underwater it gurgled, which made Ting San laugh each time. 'Huh Huh Huh' said Ting San! What a fantastic thing to have witnessed and such a smart little cookie. A shell will hold much more water each time then a curled up leaf.

To end a successful and heart-warming day I managed to make quite a good dinner that evening, consisting of veggie meat, noodles, beansprouts, mushrooms and greens cooked in a Randang Sauce and coconut cream. Very nice. I had actually made enough for tomorrows lunch and dinner too! Much more advanced in my culinary skills than when I first arrived!

The next day it rained continuously, all day. This has never happened before, normally you would get heavy downpours intermittently. However, it gave me a great excuse to crack on with paperwork, writing up my notes on enrichment, primate dietary needs, rehabilitation ideas and things I would like to continue and improve upon in the future. I plan to give a copy to Gavin or Tim, as they are the front line driving force of WOX and therefore responsible for ensuring continued support and progression of this rescue and rehabilitation centre. I am also leaving a copy of my reports for Heather, when she returns here again, as a backup. Apparently the Secretary of State will be visiting Matang on Saturday, so this is hopefully a good sign of great support from the government too.

The now dismantled cage was collected from Dianas' brother's house and we are planning to clean and disinfect it all, repaint it and then rebuild and customise it, with a view to housing Matt and Boboy, gradually integrating them for long term companionship and bonding. Macaques are very social primates and need to live with other conspecifics, exactly the same as people do.

After work Aaron, Cora and I decided to walk the trail around the centres enclosures. The entrance to the enclosures has a large green sign with a cartoon animal on it (not sure what!) which just has to be mentioned. It is written in both English and Malaysian and the English version reads as follows:

CAUTION!

Exclusion of Liabilities (Regulation No. 10 of the National Parks & Nature Reserves Regulations 1999)

"Any person visiting Matang Wildlife Centre shall enter the centre at his/her own risk. The Sarawak Government shall not be responsible for any physical, mental or emotional injury sustained or any loss of life or property whatsoever within Matang Wildlife Centre"

Controller of National Parks & Nature Reserves

Well, I think that just about covers everything!

The boardwalks were a bit lethal in the wet so maybe something needs to be done to adapt these and make them safer for visitors. Duly noted to pass on amongst my findings, although liability for any mishaps is covered in the above statement!

We all find it amazing where we are, it would be so easy to just take everything for granted and not really notice our surroundings. Something we all tend to do in our day to day lives, wherever we live.

The 2 main species of tree around the enclosure trail are Kandang Binatang (pandanus species) which occurs in Lowland Primary Forest and some open areas. This is one of around 700 species of Pandan found throughout the world and is cultivated for weaving mats, household items and headgear.

The other species of tree is Nyatoh Durian (*Palaquium gutta)* which is a medium to large sized tree, growing up to 45m tall but only around 60cm in diameter. This tree has roots above ground, called buttress roots, to support its height. Rainforest soil is poor nutritionally, so the roots do not penetrate deep into the soil but rather spread out above ground, gathering nutrients nearer the surface and acting as anchors around the tree, sometimes intertwining with roots from other trees to form a network of strong structural support. Buttress roots are hollow and so sound like natural drums when struck hard. They are real life 'jungle drums', something that chimpanzees use to their advantage when displaying strength and attitude to one another during any conflict or disagreement. The timber from these trees is used for planks and furniture making. The seeds contain a special kind of fat used for making soap, candles and also for cooking. The sap (gutta percha) is said to produce the best latex. A useful tree indeed.

Some trees have bark like camouflage combat gear, whilst others sport liana vines, hanging down like ribbons on a maypole, albeit not as colourful and a lot stiffer! Other trees are clad in huge green, succulent leaves that are bigger than both your feet when pressed together! A very lush and vibrant environment for sure.

As we neared the end of the trail, arriving at the animal centre, we came across a new type of spider . I can only liken it to a St Andrews cross type one, that puts 2 legs together with others to make a 'X' outline, and then does the same design within the web. It looks much better that way and might not be so bad for arachnaphobes to deal with, losing the 8-legged creepy crawly frightening image.

Doris and Mamu escaped again today by the way. Mamu took herself back, but Doris had other ideas and decided to pay a visit to the volunteers doing the fencing. There were no offers of help from her, just project managing I think, making sure the quality of work met her exacting standards.

Rita and Lola, who work in the offices at the Matang Visitor Centre, kindly booked a treehouse at Permai for me to stay in on Saturday night. I have always had a dream of living in a treehouse, ever since watching the Tarzan series on TV as a young girl. He had an amazing one! Incidentally, I also loved Robinson Crusoe's house he built in the original TV series. I have simple taste when it comes down to it it appears! The treehouse stay was a bit expensive for just me as they are all double roomed accommodation, but it looks absolutely amazing, and I have worked a lot lately, so this is an ideal opportunity not to be missed.

Later on, I was reading O'Hanlon's book again reminding me of all the insects I've seen here. They all appear giant sized and all seem to have the ability to fly – like the giant black flying beetles and the huge bright green flying locusts/crickets plus my favourite that I see every day – big, bright red dragonflies which are always too quick to photograph. Its like Jurassic Park for insects here. The rain was still lashing down so I fell asleep while reading on the settee. I'd become quite chilly with the rain so had switched off the ceiling fan. When I looked up at the now still blades I noticed they each had an inch long fringe of black fluff that had collected over time on them. I don't think they ever get switched off normally!

At work the following morning Keith asked if I was happy to move the quarantine macaques into their holding cages so the other volunteers could enter the enclosures safely to do the cleaning. Aqil normally has this responsibility but he had a day off. No problem I thought. Wrong! I had tested all the locks and all seemed secure but this particular one was faulty and Boboy's deft fingers and bright mind took full advantage and made short work of it. Somehow he managed to undo it, having watched the process daily for so long, and escape, making a beeline for Karen's arm. He had clearly taken umbrage over something but luckily didn't hurt her too much. A quick nip but it was enough to shake her, and the others, a fair bit. The other keepers managed to get Boboy back into his cage very quickly. It could have been so much worse. I felt sick all day, thinking about what may have been and how careless I had been not to double check. In any zoo, safari park or rescue centre situation it is general practice for one keeper to lock a padlock and another keeper to check the locks, prior to any movement of animals. This is the reason why. We still have torrential rain by the way – this is 2 whole days and nights now.

We only had to work half day as the weekend was upon us and time to take another excursion for a couple of days. Gavin drove us to Singgahsana so we could put in some laundry (it just doesn't dry well in the humid rainforests of Matang) and to do a bit of shopping in Kuching before heading off to Pantai Damai Santabong for the weekend to stay at a new resort called The Village House. Keith and Caroline have offered to keep a check on the kittens and Mum for me today and Sunday and Aqil offered to cover Saturday. I went to visit Ernesto to see about another tattoo but his shop was all closed up. Keith had tried a week or so ago with no joy. He must be having a break or at a Tattoo Convention somewhere. Maybe just as well! Instead I decided to return to Singgahsana and send an email home again. Walking into the lobby I happened to look towards the coffee bar and there, hanging above it was Heathers Rice Field Hat she had lost. Fantastic. I texted her straight away and she was over the moon, asking me to return it to Matang ready for her next visit.

The others went off and decided to get a t-shirt printed for Aqil. On the front it had a photo of us all next to the fence we had been constructing and on the back were the words "member of the G&T club"! This group had got Aqil heavily into Gin & Tonic during their stay here, not something you would think a group of volunteers at an animal rescue centre would want to achieve I wouldn't have thought.

The Village House is situated on the outskirts of Santubong village, within the foothills of Mount Santubong and is a 45 minute drive from Kuching. Hidden away behind tall gates it is a new and upmarket hotel that is just about to be opened. It is owned by Donald and Marina, the same couple who own Singghasana hostel.

We were privileged to be the first people to stay there and try it out. It looked lovely as we drove in through the outer gates around 7 o'clock that evening but, WOW, once we walked through the big wooden doors, with their driftwood handles, into the courtyard, it was unbelievable. The first thing you notice is a fully mature tree surrounded by the signature fish catching pots that had been made into lampshades. Flagstones gently swept around the tree revealing the resort stretching out before you. The central 40' long swimming pool, continually spilling over to trickle through the surrounding cobbles, is flanked either side by two large orange and terracotta 2-storey accommodation blocks, each with sweeping wooden staircases to the upper floors and wide terraces below laid out with heavy wooden furniture and, like Singgahsana, various antiquities collected by the couple during their trips around the world. These antiques included intricately carved full sized bullock carts from

India and Burma, probably 50-100 years old and used for ceremonial purposes. Also, there were several brightly coloured wooden rhinoceros hornbills (the national bird of Malaysia) of all sizes dotted around here and there and huge natural bromeliads could be seen clinging to the support pillars. Beyond the pool was a lush 'grassed' area, much more lush than the grass we know. Aaron told us that its a type of grass used in America a lot as it thrives in arid conditions. Two carved poles were set in the grass like totem poles and then, at the far end of the garden, a large raised gazebo platform, covered in bamboo matting and cushions, with a rattan roof, for relaxing in.

At the top end of the pool another 2 storey building has an upper seating area with a 20' long dining table made from a single tree slice, and a smaller room off this galleried area had a huge TV and DVD. The walls of the accommodation were corrugated metal panels with the main structure constructed of Ironwood. Couples rooms had 4-poster beds with white netting draped around the posts and top. Our dormitory room had 3 bunk beds and our own bathroom, which wouldn't have looked out of place in a 5* hotel to be honest. We had a toilet, 2 showers, each with huge oblong metal rain-shower heads, and 2 huge square basins sat on top of a long vanity unit. A wall to wall mirror above the basins and a big lower arrangement to one side completed the picture. Double wooden doors with a chunky wooden push-across latch separated the bathroom from the bedroom. A totally amazing and luxurious setting and hotel. OK, so some of it wasn't quite finished - we had wires hanging from the ceiling in the toilet and shower where lights should be but hey, it was fine. Being the first people to stay here we were the only guests so had the place totally to ourselves, free to explore and experience everything at our leisure. Our evening meal was beautifully presented and delicious, using locally sourced fresh produce. Visit http://www.villagehouse.com.my for more information and stunning pictures of this little oasis in Borneo. Sally had bought packets of glowstick bracelets earlier, in readiness for the street party on Thursday so, having some spare, we all adorned ourselves with bracelets to dress up for our opulent meal. After eating we relaxed with a few drinks, the others with their usual red wine and G&Ts whilst I had a couple of beers and a Baileys with milk (yum). Aaron and I were the last to bed around 1.30am after retiring to the TV room to watch a DVD, although the best we could come up with was 'Dirty Sanchez – the movie'! There was no rush to be up early in the morning as the group had decided to spoil themselves and have a lie in, not ordering breakfast to be served until 10am. I wanted to venture down to the sea to look for the glow-in-the-dark plankton but it was still hammering it down with rain so I chickened out. Shame.

I didn't want to get out of the amazing hot morning shower, especially as it was still lashing down outside. Surely there can't be much more rain left in the sky – we'll be flooded everywhere. After enjoying a hearty full English breakfast I said my goodbyes and checked out, ready for my onward journey to Permai Rainforest Resort where my treehouse was waiting. The others were staying here for 2-3 nights, enjoying the lap of luxury.

Alex, one of the staff here, very kindly drove me to the resort and persuaded security to let him drive me right up to the start of the pathway leading to the accommodation, as it is a bit of a hike and I would get totally drenched having to walk the whole length. Very happily the security chap said yes and provided me with a complimentary umbrella and a map for the final part of my journey.

I was booked in to Treehouse No 7 and, armed with my map and brolly off I go up the boardwalk pathway. The place is absolutely beautiful. Little bridges and concrete pathways meandered through the trees, passing a Boathouse on the beach and a covered seating area, jammed full of people and their accompanying umbrellas. Up the hill and round to the right I pass the large wooden cafe where meals are served all day (7am-10.30pm) and wonderful sunsets can be witnessed. Over another little bridge and there is No7. Three flights of steps up to the front door and in I go.

The outside of the treehouse is covered with large bark shingle panels. Inside, grooved wood panelling and a 20' high vaulted ceiling in the main area. A large double bed in the centre of the room looks out over the South China Sea through the treetops. Almost floor length windows surround the room except for double French doors facing the sea, which slide back to reveal a verandah and two chairs.

So I'm sitting on my verandah and I think I have found my paradise. Wooden treehouse in the Bornean rainforest, overlooking the sea, with stunning beaches, waterfalls and who knows what flora and fauna surrounding me. To top it off, it backs onto Mount Santabong. All I need is for the rain to stop and a stunning sunset to appear!

I couldn't wait any longer so, having got all my kit sorted, I grabbed my camera and umbrella and headed out to explore my surroundings.

The very fact that this is now the 3rd day of torrential rain has made the waterfalls absolutely humongous. I was feeling I'd lost out not doing Kubah waterfall or the Matang waterfall trail but this really makes up for it. I came across 3 raging streams coming down from the mountain and into the sea.

One of the mountain streams had been harnessed into a Jungle Pool, a raised wooden platform of two pools, diverted for our pleasure, before overflowing back onto its route to the sea.

Beach 2, as it was called on the map, was as beautiful as the beach at Bako. Rocks and boulders of all different colours and sizes, holes and channels gouged into them by the sea over time. The mist hung in the canopy of the trees and deep gullies cut through the sand. I couldn't take enough pictures! The umbrella did a fine job of keeping me and the camera dry.

I retraced my steps, after writing "Borneo" in the sand (and taking a photo of it), trying to make it sink in where I actually am. A dream come true. I headed down to the little shop at the entrance ready to buy lots of souvenirs and a book on what plants and animals could be seen around here. Very disappointingly there were no such things. The usual SFC Polo shirts and tote bags, some snacks and other touristy t-shirts. Books on plants and animals of Borneo in general and books on Bako and Gudang Mulu but not even a leaflet on this place. Very disappointed. Determined to buy something and support the resort, I bought a pack of 4 notelets with pencil drawings of gibbons on, some cheese snacks and a small bar of chocolate, then headed back to my little house in the trees. As I mentioned before, I always loved Tarzan's house on telly so wanted my own, just for one day. Eventually, about 5.30pm it actually stopped raining.

As the night obscured my view I settled down to sleep, hoping the rain stays stopped so I can explore and visit the nearby Cultural Village tomorrow. With the verandah doors open (mosquito-net screens shut!) and air-con off I fell asleep to the sound of crashing waves and the feel of sea breeze on my face. Much better than dusty fan blades whooping round. The bed appeared damper than usual but I had come to accept the fact that everything around you is soggy and musty by now. That's humid rainforest life for you.

I got up at sunrise wanting to experience my perfect world awaken alongside me and decided to do the 1½ hour forest trail before heading down to the cafe for breakfast. There were 2 routes to follow, the Red Trail being only 30 minutes and the Blue Trail the longer one. Just as I began walking a tree came crashing down by the stream to my right! Not a great start. Next, I hit an obstacle on the Blue Trail – how to cross the raging waters following the 3 days of torrential rain. Having only sandals on and sporting my last plaster, where I scuffed the skin off my big toe moving a chair Friday at Santubong, I thought that it might be wise to admit defeat on this one. I was very disappointed but decided I would be able to still do the Red Trail. I was wrong to assume this would be a leisurely amble through the forest however as it turned out I had many water crossings that way, with ropes strung across to hold onto. There were also handy ropes strung throughout the trail, to help scramble my way up banks and over boulders. I did really enjoy this walk through the forest and, being early morning I was hoping to see lots of wildlife. Sadly I didn't although I could hear some different birds. The trail finished up at the assault course that had been erected for kids to play on by beach No2 so, being close to home, I popped into my treehouse for a hot shower and change of clothes before breakfast. Still a little early to eat I checked out the beach in front of my house, which had huge amazing boulders on it layered in colours of pink, yellow and black, pitted with age old wear from the sea looking like chunks of cinder toffee. One of the boulders was so large it had a deep hollow filled with crystal clear sea water and lots of pebbles on the bottom. After a while wandering amongst these marvels of time, and being thankful that the rain had actually held out overnight and this morning, I headed for breakfast. This was included in the price of the stay and consisted of sausage, egg, hash brown and tomato, which was gorgeous, followed by 2 slices of toast and Kaya – a local speciality of coconut jam. It was fantastic, and I don't even eat jam. I vowed I must try to find some to take home for everyone. Since that time I can now get Coconut Jam here in the UK, including one with chocolate in, both of which are vegan (as I am now), and absolutely divine.

After my hearty breakfast I had a chance to grab an hours' doze on my bed up in the trees before it was time to leave my paradise. I have had a whole 24 hours so it was well worth the RM188 which, although expensive compared to the Backpackers Longhouse here at RM20, or Singgahsana at RM30, its still only about £25 real money. When I went to check out they kindly actually only charged me RM160 as I was alone, which was really lovely of them.

It was a 5 minute walk down the road to the Sarawak Cultural Village where I spent the rest of the day. The heavens opened as soon as I walked through the gates and continued on and off all day but I managed just fine using rainy opportunities to visit the different examples of full sized replica buildings or by making use of the umbrella the previous volunteers had left for me. I laughed at the time. I mean, me, with a pink brolly?! I had used the courtesy one provided at Permai Rainforest Resort whilst I stayed there but I was jolly glad of the girls' pink one now.

Sarawak Cultural Village opened in 1991 and is a 'village within a village' with a thriving community of staff and performers actually living there. The village is set within 17½ acres of beautifully landscaped gardens, centred around a lake, which is there to represent the rivers which are the lifeline of all of these cultures, thereby signifying the importance of water to the 7 differing cultures of Sarawak represented in this living village. These 7 cultures are Bidayu, Iban, Penan, Orang Ulu, Melanau, Malay and Chinese.

When you first enter the gates you are presented with a Passport, which you will get stamped at each house and building you visit as you make your way around the village. The longhouses and other replica buildings are truly wonderful, and each house has differing arts and skills to show you, displayed by tribes people in traditional dress. You really feel you have stepped back in time and are experiencing the Borneo that you have read about and imagine still today.

In the Bidayu house I had the chance to try my hand at the blowpipe. I hit the target so, feeling rather proud and pleased with myself, I bought a souvenir blowpipe, complete with a little spearhead mounted on the end and a decorated canister complete with little darts. I also persuaded the chap to kindly throw in a bracelet for me.

My next stop was the Melanau Tall House *(Rumah Tinggi)*, an extremely large wooden house with a central staircase taking you up to the living quarters above. Most Melanau are farmers and fishermen but they also produce Sago so, after watching some of the process required to extract sago from tree logs to create little beads of Sago used for cooking into cakes or serving with fish and vegetables (similar to cous cous) I bought some Sago crackers and Sago mixed with coconut and brown sugar, which can be eaten as is or recommended as delicious when banana is dipped in and eaten. Sounded good to me.

Visiting each house twice then made perfect time for me to catch the 4pm cultural show in the theatre, which had very comfy sofa chairs rather than hard theatre seats. The show was incredibly colourful and beautiful, telling traditional stories through magical and mesmerising performances. Mr Boon, our trusty taxi driver, was as reliable as ever and waiting at the gates after the show to drive me back to Matang ready for my return to work duties tomorrow.

When I arrived back at the street, Sally and Penny were also home from Santabong but the 2 couples had decided to stay at Singgahsana tonight, back in Kuching.

I couldn't find the kittens when I first got home but eventually found that Mum had moved them to a box under the sink, amongst the cleaning products! I tried to move the feline family back to the bedroom but she was having none of it. I left them be.

"Wandering re-establishes the original harmony which once existed between man and the universe"

Anatole France

CHAPTER FOURTEEN

"There are no foreign lands. It is the traveller only who is foreign"

Robert Louis Stevenson

The rain returned with a vengeance, raining all morning practically, so I stayed under cover and started to rub down and paint the panels of the rescued macaque cage. Sally set to work routing out a brilliant wooden plaque with all our names on, to go on the fence that was now completed and then carried on to do a little name plaque for each of the quarantine animals too.

The keepers were instructed to pull another of their antics on us today. Without a word to Keith, it was decided to open up the divides and mix all of the 6 macaques on the hill together and leave them to just get along. This is absolute madness and could have gone so very, very wrong. Fortunately it didn't, in the short term at least, although the two youngest, Chick and Baby, were not happy and Kevin was now very nervous. This has spoilt any chance we had of integrating Juan with the girls. He is a recent addition and only a baby so it would have been ideal for him to integrate with the 3 girls and learn from them, ready for release as a group. He is too young to breed for a few years yet so would be able to be released and given the opportunity to stabilise before breeding naturally in the wild. Talking of which, Tammy is in season so tension and hormones are going to be raging, resulting most probably with captive born babies, making rehabilitation and release of the boys, as well as the girls, very difficult for them and for us.

Another big event today was a new Manager of the place taking over. The good news is he is highly qualified in the fields of conservation & animal welfare, with a desire to make MWC a centre of excellence. This is great news and I really hope he is able to achieve this. I believe he studied at Oxford Brookes.

I tried moving the kittens from the cleaning product box again but no – mum moved them straight back again.

One thing that really cheered me up at the end of the day. I went to check on the macaques last thing, and there was Emily, proudly sitting **inside** her house. She looked dry and cosy, out of the rain bless her.

Have I mentioned the favourite colour scheme of buildings around these parts of the world seems to be orange and green. Maybe the colours are significant, or maybe it is just hard to find any other colours of paint. Either way it does look rather nice.

Ginj has informed me she will not be coming to meet me when I get home as she can't face going without fags for the 3 or 4 hours travelling. Dad and Mum are kindly picking me up from the airport and Ginj will be staying at home. Bit miffed about this to be honest as I would have thought I would rank a little bit above a couple of cigarettes. Apparently not.

The main activity of Day 57 was to gut Juan's cage and put all new ropes and toys in for him, hoping to stop some of his stereotypic cycle of behaviour and snap him out of his trance-like existence. Any animal or person in a stressful environment with no stimulation will resort to stereotypic behaviours of some description which can be extremely difficult to break out of once entrenched – like an all consuming OCD. Our efforts worked and he loved it, testing each bit of his new home over and over all day. Really well worth it. We need to do Boboy next.

We actually got treated to a nice bit of hot sunshine today, which was marvellous and the afternoon was spent shopping – for the last time. I actually took a video of the drive to the shops, including the roadside grass cutter team, as a reminder of the scenery and overall feel of Kuching, and Sarawak as a whole, my home for the past 2½ months. I will miss this place that's for sure, although one thing about Borneo I won't miss is the insects. I'm so fed up with mosquitos eating me, ants all over the kitchen units and, worst of all, fishing weevils out of my cereal bowl each morning before adding milk!

Tim had organised a night-time forest trek for this group, as he had done for the last one, with a camp out at the forest base overnight. No-one wanted to go though, other than Penny so I did feel sorry for Tim, having to go as promised, but only having one person for company. Such a shame for both of them.

Arriving at work the next morning I found a HUGE cicada (unfortunately dying) – I would never imagine an insect could be that big. The body itself would be about half the size of an A5 sheet of paper. Amazing, but I wouldn't want to be attacked by one! It could not be saved and so once it had died we gave it to Matt the macaque for some natural enrichment. He absolutely loved it and relished this exquisite addition to his daily diet. It must have taken him about 15 minutes to eat it but he ate it all, apart from two gossamer wings, one large one and one smaller one.

All the keepers got on board today, helping us to erect the newly painted rescued macaque cage. It was good to see them all working alongside our guys and being enthusiastic. A great team effort.

Later, I had another small victory, getting mum cat to accept the kittens being out of the cleaning products box by setting them up under my dressing table. They were hidden away all safe and secure but in a much more healthy environment. It was also good to see they were starting to move around a bit. Happy with this new arrangement I then went over to Karen, Gary and Sally's to look at their end-of-stay presentation to the management team tomorrow. I stayed a while but they were all drinking, silly and crude. I can't be doing with it and am dreading the farewell party planned for tomorrow.

A much better way to spend the evening was by joining Aaron and Cora, secretly painting the bear enclosure wall as a surprise for Keith and Caroline. Apparently Aaron had started last night and they let me in on it. Great to be a part of getting that done so the bears could soon be able to move in to a proper enclosure and feel grass under their feet and see the sky above their heads. What a wonderful couple of people these two are.

We were having problems with the bung in Matty the crab-eating macaques water bowl. There are no sink plugs or anything like it here so to make a watertight bung you need to shape a piece of wood into a pointed cone type shape which fits snugly into the drainage hole, expanding when wet and thus preventing the water from escaping. Matt's would not stop leaking, probably because of the wood degrading over time, so we constantly had to check he had drinking water throughout the day, which was not ideal for him. In the short term I decided to give him Boboys big water butt for a change. We hadn't actually used it with water in for Boboy, just as a piece of enrichment furniture in his enclosure but for Matt we filled it completely with water. He absolutely loved it, and thinking about it I should've done it much sooner. He is a crab-eating macaque and so is happy in water, diving for crabs. To watch him keep diving to the bottom, swimming around and resurfacing, happily gasping for breath and soaking wet, was absolutely fantastic. It brought a lump to the throat to see him so very happy. This is a totally natural behaviour which automatically kicked in, even if he was restricted to diving down into a water butt and not able to actually swim any length, just in a tight circle. I fashioned him a new wooden bung for his water trough so we shall see if he still has drinking water in the morning.

The rest of the volunteers had been busy using a router to carve out names on little wooden signs for all quarantine animals. We put up the ones for Matt and Juan and they looked really good, giving the monkeys a personality and making it more natural for people to take to them as characters and talk to them, using their names. Once the signs were complete we all chipped in and actually finished painting the bear enclosure walls. This is the first enclosure to have every outside wall painted and I must say it looks mighty fine, giving the animals a sense of distance and extended scenery all around, rather than hot, high, blank concrete walls.

WOX had arranged for a photographer to spend time with us, taking pictures all day for their website apparently. He was a very nice, smiley chap and very polite. We nicknamed him "Shake Hands Man" from the old Japanese-based TV series "Banzai" - in which a roving reporter was tasked with trying to continue to shake hands with a famous celebrity for as long as possible before the celebrity became uncomfortable and pulled their hand away. The name fitted him very well. Sadly, we never got to know his proper name.

Our very productive day was completed by making a couple of toys for Boboys enclosure and stocking up the Behavioural Enrichment freezer with goodies, in readiness for our departure and the arrival of a fresh group of volunteers. We are hoping they will carry it on. The keepers finished putting the new enclosure together. It just needs concreting in place and setting up as a new home for another rescued monkey. Good job done. The Sun continued to shine throughout the morning but then turned to rain all afternoon, which was a shame for the volunteers leaving party tonight.

Sitting on my verandah after work I saw a pair of birds I had never noticed here before. They had a lovely song to them, were quite small, and black and white in colour. Caroline informed me that they were called Magpie Robins. Also, on my back porch was quite a thick, shiny bronze lizard. Really shimmery and beautiful but I couldn't get to my camera in time to capture it and look it up in any books sadly.

The normal silly street music was going on, breaking my serene oneness with the natural world around me, so I put my MP3 headphones on until it was time to head out for the party.

The party was actually a huge success and it did stop raining which was lovely. Karen, Sally and Cora had prepared lots of amazing food, I'd wrapped 4 pass the parcels, and we all had balloons and glowsticks. The cafeteria was the perfect setting, with bags of room for the food, the BBQ to be set up and for games to be played. All the local families had joined us so the atmosphere was wonderful with children laughing and playing, men doing the BBQ and sorting out the rice wine, women getting a chance to relax and chat. The families had also brought food to add to the table so we had chicken pieces, chicken in bamboo, rice leaf parcels, pink blancmange – which was eaten along with the savoury stuff!! Everyone was there – all the keepers and their wives and children, the girls from the office and one of their mother in laws, Aquil, Keith, Caroline, all us volunteers and Tim joined us later.

Karen and Gary had made sure we all contributed the same amount of money to the party fund prior to them going shopping for the goodies. The main bulk of the money went on the G&T club t-shirts, spirits and some beers. I wasn't having a t-shirt or spirits so childishly tried to make sure I got my 'money's worth' throughout the night by drinking as much beer as I could! This also had the downside that I then proceeded to have a cigarette to accompany the alcohol. I really paid for this later, and it served me right really. Once I returned to my Bilik, the room was spinning, I felt sick and I didn't know where on earth I was. I felt so drunk and ill. At one point I was trying to climb through the back of the wardrobe to get to the bathroom! I felt like I was in Narnia but there were no soft coats to climb through! Eventually I made it to the bathroom intact! What a state to be in. I have never been a heavy drinker and should have known better, especially in the humidity of a rainforest.

The following morning, boy did I still feel rough. I was continually throwing up and the room was still spinning. I really couldn't make it for work AT ALL, which made me feel so bad as it was these volunteers' last day. They came back to check on me at 10am, to see if I wanted to come to their presentation but I just couldn't do it. It turned out that no-one from Sarawak Forestry Commission or Tim could make it to listen to their presentation either as a conference had apparently run over. Understandably they were all a bit upset by that, having worked so hard on it. In the end they were able to gather all the office staff along with Keith, Caroline and Ting San as a worthy and appreciative audience.

Caroline and Cora persuaded me to go down and join them for the group photo on the steps of the admin building and to then receive my souvenir certificate of attendance as a volunteer and a leaving card. The card was absolutely lovely, as Caroline had written a really nice message inside and it had a copy of a hilarious Borneo newspaper clipping on the front which showed a photo of Johnny & Judy the Samba Deer. The article went on to explain that "Johnny was the one with the Antelopes"! What they meant to say was "antlers!! Cracking, so funny, I shall keep that card always.

I was still very woozy so returned back to my bilik for another lie down. Meanwhile, a Crocodile had been rescued from some local sewers and brought to Matang. The others went to see it arrive but I decided not to as, firstly, I still felt rough and secondly we didn't know what sort of state it would be in, it would be extremely stressed with people milling around and we were not sure how they intended to deal with it.

The working day finished at 2pm with the volunteers heading into Kuching, and Singgahsana. I waited until later, going in at 4pm with Keith and Caroline.

The final meal was arranged for us to go to Top Spot, on top of the multi-storey car park. I stuck to vegetarian food and no alcohol, although Gary and Karen were up to their old tricks, trying to get us to share the bills equally all night. I was having none of it as they were drinking RM30 shorts whilst I had ONE soft drink, costing RM5!!

After the meal Tim very kindly produced a small little box for each of us. He said this was our going away present and he recommended that we take it. This had not been given to the previous group so I was a little confused but when we discovered what 'memento' was in the little boxes we didn't know if he was joking or not. We had all been supplied with worming tablets!! Whether anyone did take them or not, I don't know. I didn't. We then moved on to a different venue underneath the Top Spot building, called Garden Hill Bar, which was really nice. I had coffee!! Aaron decided to try a dessert which intrigued us. It was called "Chocolate milk tea pudding" but turned out to be just a two-tone tasteless junket effort.

Everyone was ribbing me about the wardrobe fiasco so now I'm either 'normal Marcia' or 'Narnia Marcia', dependent on whether I'm focussing on the conversation or not!

Returning to Singgahsana bar to finish off the night, I had a small glass of water and managed to carry on til around 1am but by then I had had enough and slipped off to bed.

Still feeling ropey when I woke up, I tried to eat a bit of toast but couldn't hack it. Waving off Sally I then sent an email home and checked on Ernesto for that one final tattoo and to show Cora and Aaron as they were interested in getting one from him too. When we arrived at his address the door grill was open but the sign on the door stated that he doesn't actually open until 11am. Cora and Aaron are not flying until tonight so they were happy to go and check on him again later. I got a lift back to MWC with Tim and Lisa, did a load of washing (as its unbelievably hot today so hoping to get it dried nicely) and then headed into work for the last hour. I found myself feeling better as the day went on but any time I attempted to eat sent me back downhilll again. Returning home I fell asleep on the sofa until 7.30pm then rallied myself rather hastily as I realised it was raining again now so I needed to rescue my washing.

Caroline and I worked the following day but what a pair we were! I'm still not able to eat and keep it in, and am light-headed and hot. Caroline is also light-headed and hot but with an all over rash to boot! Ting San is fine!

We spent the morning on the platform in the forest, Ting San being very gently attentive to my legs and arms. She has a little way of rubbing her wrist on yours then does like a Chinese burn – don't know why, or if this is something any other orangutan would do. Can't imagine what runs through her little head sometimes. She brought me a leaf to put water in it for her, but then when I produced my water bottle for the task in hand she promptly just nabbed my water bottle and helped herself! Such a bright and cheeky little girl.

Diana came by to visit the macaques she had donated from her brother and to wish me and Caroline all the best as we won't see her again. She asked us to contact her if ever we returned though which was lovely. A really nice lady.

I finished writing up all my notes and training manuals to leave for WOX/SFC – Caroline kindly typed it all up for me. We arranged my last working day to be Wednesday when I would then spend the final evening and night at Caroline and Keith's house. The plan was for me to get a Taxi from their house into Kuching for some last minute present shopping during the final day and then they would drive in to meet me, bringing my luggage from their house, pick me up from town and take me to the airport. This was so good of them considering all they have to deal with themselves. Their last day here is Friday, which will be really difficult after 3 years, and no-one around to help them as they have helped me.

Caroline went the doctors about her rash as it wasn't clearing up and also she still has a fever. She was given steroids to hopefully combat the problem. With Caroline away from work, Ting San was being stubborn again and wouldn't go into the forest with either Joseph or Keith. I had to carry her up there and stay for a while. Whenever I went to leave she noticed and chased after me so I had to wait until she went high up into canopy before I was able to sneak off! She has touched and affected so many people so deeply, I just hope people can give her a dream life in return.

I actually counted the steps to the top of the bears today. Its 88 quite uniform ones following the trail route or, from the Macaques, its 86 of varying depths, 70 of which take you to the proposed new macaque enclosure and half of them are knee high on me and I'm 5'8"! What chance would the macaques seriously get of being fed even once every day, let alone twice a day, not to mention added enrichment visits if they do get moved to this new enclosure?! I really hope they do though.

The rest of the morning was spent making and handing out enrichment, chilling with the animals, listening to the constant 'telexes' being sent by the Cicadas, and to the song of the Bulbul (a medium sized passerine songbird). Also I thought how strange and tiny English leaves are going to look (if there are any still on trees when I return home, being Winter!). I stayed at work late, making stuff to re-furbish Boboy's enclosure tomorrow, not wanting to tear myself away, knowing somehow that I probably will never get the chance to return. Cora texted me to say she was really missing the place, especially Matt the macaque.

Giving Leah the keys to both biliks she was like a kid in a sweet shop bless her!! Checking out all the goodies that had been left behind by the volunteers. Food that had not been used, clothes that would be pointless taking back home, toiletries etc. I love that nothing will go to waste.

On that final morning of working a full day I walked straight past Aqil sitting on the patio in the animal centre. He had shaved all his hair off and so I didn't recognise him at all. He looked like a little buddhist monk, sat cross legged on the floor, grinning away at me. He and I spent the morning re-furbishing Boboy, including a water butt to swim and dive in, so that is now all the macaques and gibbons done, which I am really happy about. It is nice to see Boboy relaxed again, now all the volunteers have gone. He's such a lovely little boy with no stress, but can get anxious when there are a lot of people and noise around the place sometimes. A sensitive little soul really.

I feel I have had the opportunity to totally make a difference during my time here. The new boss man (just never remember his name – Abang I think) thanked me for all my work and said I would be welcome back anytime, and to keep in touch with any further ideas and recommendations I may have, which was really comforting to hear. It gave me confidence that Matang will continue to progress well now that he has taken over as he has animal keeping experience aplenty. Apparently he worked at Jersey Zoo and is aware of many other English zoos too. He's a good man, with the passion to go alongside his experience.

Tim turned up today so I was able to have discussions with him about the Behavioural Enrichment, the manuals

I have written and how Aqil can carry on as volunteer co-ordinator, to ensure enrichment and animal welfare continues.

This is my last night on the street. Packing up all my possessions, and doing a final load of washing, listening to that damned awful music one final time! I can't even shut it out by closing the door because we have no walls at the top! I really couldn't stand any more nights of it I don't think. I submit – totally. Putting on my headphones I went through my MP3 and selected a 'best of Borneo' playlist of my own songs which ended up as amazing and finished my night off perfectly.

I thought to myself - Don't be sad its over, be glad you were here and did it.

I tried not to think about my last day at work too much! Going over the Behavioural Enrichment with Aqil, doing one more circuit of the trail as we went, discussing what the enrichment was for and how to assess and document each items' individual success with the differing species. This included how long it took to make something, compared to how long the item was actually enjoyed by the animal who received it. Did it replicate any natural behaviours? Did it use the correct muscle groups for the individual task at hand? How did it benefit the animal physically, nutritionally and mentally? All vital questions when thinking of enrichment for any animal in any captive setting.

I then spent most of the final afternoon in the company of my favourites, the gibbons and the macaques. I am so fond of these guys and will definitely miss them, but plan to keep in touch and up to speed with their progress when I return home.

After work it was time to move out of Aqil's house so he can return home at last whilst I move on to stay at Keith and Caroline's for my final night in Borneo. We decided on a takeaway supper which was Nee Goreng. We had actually planned Satay but, after stopping by the shop to order it, Keith had gone off to get the rice from another seller and when he returned to the Satay man, it was all closed up, although the kitchen fire was still burning! The Nee Goreng went down very well though as we sat watching DVDs of Keith's photographs he had taken during their time at Matang. They were fantastic pictures and Keith kindly gave me a copy of his disc. I didn't sleep much as it was very hot and my mind was whirring like a good 'un.

We all had a bit of a lay-in then drove into Kuching for me to do shopping and for Keith and Caroline to pick up the keys to an apartment in Santabong they are being loaned for a couple of days, until they too fly back to the UK. Their last day at work is tomorrow so it will be good to stay somewhere different and take their minds off it, rather than stay in the same house they had been living in whilst working at Matang.

I stayed in Kuching until around 3pm that day, getting presents for everyone back home and having a lovely lunch out at the James Brooke Bistro on Jalan Tunku Abdul Rahman, situated along the waterfront. I had never been there for a meal before but had fancied trying it, being a round, open fronted wooden building with a colonial pavillion style and set in very lush gardens with shortly cropped lawn, cobbled stone pathways and 3 wooden steps leading into the seating area. The food was indeed very nice, serving western food and local specialities. As I sat eating my meal I watched as two gardeners were busy making sure the grounds were pristine. Despite the heat and humidity they were covered from head to toe in clothing. This was to ensure they did not got a Sun tan. In Asian cultures people strive to stay as pale-skinned as possible as this signifies you work indoors in a higher status position. If you have dark skin it tends to mean you work outside on tasks which are perceived as more 'menial' than office based work. I found this whenever I travelled around Asia. Of course, it is also much more healthy to avoid excess sunlight which can damage the skin irreparably. Incidentally, James Brooke was a soldier with the East India Company and later became an adventurer, discovering the Sarawak area of Borneo and liking it there. He therefore became the first White Rajah who founded and ruled the kingdom of Sarawak and was apparently very sympathetic and supportive of the indigenous people, being much revered by the Dayaks and Malay people. He ruled from 1841 to 1868, when he died.

I did try Ernesto's studio one more time but to no avail – I am clearly not meant to have that 3rd tattoo.

Change of plan as Keith and Caroline were still working at Matang, I returned to their house via taxi. I had to have a different taxi driver than usual, Mr Boon was already booked. He was a very nice, softly spoken chap, but we did get a bit lost looking for the house. I had the address written down on a piece of paper but it didn't seem to help him much and I couldn't remember which way to go. Nevertheless we managed to get there eventually, giving me enough time to get showered and sorted before they got back from their afternoon at work.

Driving me to the airport they very kindly stayed to keep me company until it was nearly time for my flight. It was very sad saying goodbye but still not really acknowledging that this is the end of my adventure, and theirs in a couple of days time. Again, we kept telling each other not to be sad that its ended, but to be happy that we've had the experience.

My flight was on time and off I went to Kuala Lumpur. It was a good flight too, taking 1hr 40mins and I then remembered the route using the little train to the main terminal. My second flight was a little delayed but eventually took off for home at 1am. It was a bit of a bumpy ride so I felt a bit icky (I'm not good with turbulence!) but the time didn't go too bad and, despite my little screen not working on the head rest in front of me, it was just another 2½ hrs to go, in the 12½ hr flight before I even realised so I must have dozed off really well between meals. There was a bit of drama when a couple were arrested on our plane before we could get off but, at last, it was time. I was home. 3ºC outside and 6.30am UK time.

Making my way through to collect my baggage, and then through Customs I was glad to be on solid ground once more and looking forward to seeing the smiley faces of my Mum and Dad to welcome me home. Goodness knows how early they had to get up to drive to the airport and get me. At last, there they were, waving and calling my name as I walked into the arrival area. And would you know it, Ginj was there too. She had been joking about not coming to meet me, and had brought me some warm clothes to put on. It was so nice to see their little faces again and, although feeling rather alien and tired, I was suddenly glad to be back. Driving home you realise just how beautiful your own country is. We tend to take it all for granted and not really SEE or experience our own surroundings as much as we do when we go away on holiday or something. It is just 'there', and sometimes we complain about our weather (well, its a national pastime actually!) but one thing I did appreciate was a breeze of fresh air, the different shades of green in the fields, the hedgerows, the trees and also just appreciating the familiar surroundings like a warm, cosy blanket. I've had a great time, and I know I will feel weird going into our shops, using our money, hearing English accents spoken everywhere and maybe the same old conversations, but its great to be home!

The whole object of travel is not to set foot on foreign land;
It is at last to set foot on one's own country as a foreign
land"

G.K. Chesterton

FOOTNOTES

I resumed my animal keeper job in Woburn Safari Park upon my return and wrote an article about my time in Borneo for the staff newsletter. I will always be grateful to the management at the time for allowing me the opportunity to fulfill my dream of helping rescue animals in-situ in a place that held a fascination for me, Borneo.

I haven't as yet managed to return to Borneo, although I would love to. Instead I travelled to several other countries in the following years, assisting at other animal rescue centres around the world. My next book will follow my 6 month journey through Sulawesi, Thailand, Laos, Cambodia & Singapore over a longer period of time and, if you would like to join me on that journey you will learn of my 3 near death experiences whilst in Sulawesi! A most memorable, but again wonderful, trip.

Although the bears' outside enclosure was finished whilst I was at Matang Wildlife Centre, the inside enclosures still needed completing so we didn't get to experience the release of the quarantine bears whilst there. However, shortly after we left this was achieved and I was able to watch them explore for the first time courtesy of YouTube. You can see it too by searching for "Borneo Orangutan Volunteer: Sun Bears see the Sun" 2008. I wept with joy watching it, just so moving and so privileged to have been a small part of it.

Other clips on YouTube worth looking at are Doris the Orangutan up to her escapologist antics on "Borneo Orangutan Volunteer: Still tempting Doris back in" 2008. Also, my own clip of Ting San in the just completed nursery enclosure, playing in the water at "Orangutan Angel" 2008.

OTHER REFERENCES:

"Borneo Inspired Guesthouse by Borneo Art Collective"

"Wild About Kuching" painted by local artist Leonard Siaw.

Book: Nick Garbutt, Wild Borneo (New Holland, 2006)

Book: "Into the Heart of Borneo" by Redmond O'Hanlon

I hope you have enjoyed my little book. Thank you so very much for your support. Others are in the pipeline if there is an interest, the next one of which sees me in mortal danger a couple of times!!

GLOSSARY OF SOME IBAN/MALAY WORDS

MAKAI	Eat up
ALA MALOO	Don't be shy
JAI	Bad!
SELAMAT PAGI	Good Morning
SELAMAT DATANG	Welcome
SELAMAT JALAN	Goodbye (Good Journey) – said TO someone who is leaving
SELAMAT TINGGAL	Goodbye (Good stay) – said BY someone who is leaving
TERIMA KASIH	Thankyou
AWAS	Caution (on road signs etc)
SAMA SAMA	Same same!
TABOH	Traditional Iban music
NEGARA	National
RINGGIT	Malaysian currency

IBAN phrases relating to times of sunrise and before:

Dini Ari Dalam	= Dawn deep down
Empliau Bebungi	= The calling of the gibbons
Tampak Tanah	= To see the ground

ANIMALS AT MATANG DURING MY TIME THERE

ORANGUTANS:	Aman, Chiam, Ghanti, Doris, Mamu, Ting San
GIBBONS:	Emily, Theresa
PIG-TAILED MACAQUES:	Oliver, Kevin, Chick, Juan, Dodd, Tammy, Baby
LONG TAILED MACAQUES:	Matt, Boboy, John Travolta, Sandy
DEER:	Tim, Simon, plus 2 in with Doris and a separate small herd
SUN BEARS:	Bernie, Situ, Jo, Corinne, Gummy Bear + 3 others
COCKATOO:	Thea
PORCUPINES	x2
BINTURONG	x2
CIVET	x1
LESSER ADJUTANT STORK	x2
BUFFY FISH OWL	x1
BRAHMINY KITE	x1
SOFT BACKED TURTLE	x1
LEOPARD CATS	x3
Plus	
SALT WATER CROCS	
FRESH WATER CROCS (False Gharial)	
CHICKENS	(on and off as these were food for crocodiles etc!)

SOUNDTRACK OF MY JOURNEY
(all available on YouTube I believe)

A song for the lovers	Richard Ashcroft
Wicked Game	Him
Drink you pretty	Placebo
Brother	The Organ
Nothing was special	Lendi Vexer
Explode	Uh Huh Her
Heroin Chic	The Silk Demise
Set the fire to the third bar	Snow Patrol ft Martha Wainwright
Kill 100 (Carl Craig remix)	X-Press 2
Vespertine	Ozark Henry
Running up that hill	Placebo
Runabout (Zick remix)	Little Dragon
Armagiddeon Time	The Clash
No Wow	The Kills
People are strange	Johnny Hollow
Androgyny	Garbage
Bongo Bong	Manu Chao
Trophy	Bat for lashes
Comatose	Cinephile
Move a little closer	Sonique
Breathe me	Horse
Precious pain	Melissa Etheridge
Why go?	Faithless ft Boy George
Beautiful eyes	Rita Lynch
Empty (Hideaway)	Sonique
For you	Silverfall
When doves cry	Patti Smith
Live with me	Massive Attack ft Terry Callier
Horse and I	Bat For Lashes

White Rabbit	Blue Man Group ft Esthero
I drive alone	Esthero
It will all make sense in the morning	Halou
Twenty years	Placebo
Trouble every day	Tindersticks

There was one other song but I didn't note down the artist or title and can't find it anywhere online sadly. It was one of my favourites too!